PHILIPPIANS FOR MISSIONARIES

JANAY ABALE

To all God's beautiful feet all over the world.
Keep marching.
Romans 10:15

Table of Contents

Introduction

When I was eight years old, I attended a Christian school. One day, a missionary shared during our weekly chapel service. He showed us slide after slide of a far-off people group he was trying to reach with the gospel. They were so different from me, and the people looked strange and scary to my young mind.

Terror welled up in my heart. I knew Christians were supposed to share the gospel. That meant *I* was supposed to share the gospel, but there was *no way* possible that I could *ever* do what this man was doing. I was so painfully shy I didn't even want people to look at me!

Quaking, I slid down in my seat (trying to hide from God) and vehemently told God I would *never* be a missionary.

But God's plans won out, and I'm so glad they did.

Over the next twenty years, God took me on a journey of missionary baby steps, first to Mexico, then to Haiti, Uganda, and back to Haiti again. Each little taste left me wanting more.

On my third trip to Haiti, I moved out into the village with my teammates. We pushed through shoulder-high grass as we climbed a hill. When we emerged from the grass at the top of the hill, we turned to follow the ridge. Small valleys and lazy hills stretched out in front of us, *rise, dip, rise, dip*, all velvet green under the bluest expanse of heaven.

Brown huts sprinkled the hillsides, each representing souls that needed Jesus. They needed the Savior.

The thought burned within me.

I looked up at the clouds as Scripture proclaiming God's majesty exploded in my heart.

Was there any more significant purpose in life than to proclaim the glory of the Savior, who came in human flesh and dwelt among us to deliver us from the penalty of our sins and give us life more abundantly?

I could think of nothing else.

The gospel became a consuming passion in my heart, and I actively sought people with whom to share it. I witnessed on the streets of Skid Row in Los Angeles, served in the Children's Ministry, and volunteered in the church's missions office.

I wanted to *go*. To speak. To make Jesus known.

What a drastic change was wrought in me through the Holy Spirit!

I was living out what Paul describes in Philippians 1:13: "For it is God who works in you, both to will and to work for his good pleasure."

His passions had become my passions. He had put His desires into my heart. I now wanted what God wanted.

Two years after that trip to Haiti, I quit my job as a middle school English teacher, packed up my life, and moved overseas as a missionary to Uganda. This was the first place I had ever shared the gospel, trembling in front of over a hundred high school students.

I'm currently in my eleventh year on the mission field, and the book of Philippians is even more meaningful to me now when I read it in light of my mission experience. I see the heart of Paul, the missionary, in every word. He treasured the gospel and gave his life to make salvation known to all men. He faced myriad challenges in the process but chose to "press on toward the goal" (Phil. 3:14) and remained faithful to his calling.

How did Paul persevere despite hardships, imprisonment, beatings, slander, conflict with co-workers, riots, and near-death experiences? How can we remain faithful despite our own challenges?

King Solomon said, "There's nothing new under the sun" (Eccl. 1:9). The modern world has provided new modes of transportation and communication for missionaries, but the spiritual principles of making disciples of all nations haven't changed. Paul's attitudes, advice, and example are still applicable today.

In this Deep Dive Devotional, we will approach the book of Philippians with the eyes of a missionary and apply the Scripture to our gospel work. Regardless of where your mission field may be, Philippians will encourage, challenge, and strengthen you for the work at hand.

Background For the Book of Philippians

PHILIPPI

The city of Philippi, situated on a major trade route about ten miles from the Aegean Sea, was a Roman colony. This meant that Philippi adhered to Roman law, customs, and culture, making it a significant part of the Roman Empire. Archeologists excavated the city's ruins and discovered a theater, acropolis, forum, and baths, all of which were standard features for a Roman city.

Paul visited Philippi on his second missionary journey and, moved by the people's faith, planted a church there (Acts 16).

PAUL'S IMPRISONMENT AND THE PURPOSE OF THE LETTER

About ten years after planting the church in Philippi, Paul was imprisoned for preaching the gospel, which happened to him several times. Usually, Paul supported himself through the work of his own hands. A tent-maker by trade, it was his custom not to receive financial support from the churches he ministered to (1 Thess. 2:9). However, he did make some exceptions, and this letter to the Philippians is in response to one of those times.

The Philippian church heard of Paul's arrest and his imprisonment. Knowing he was in need, they sent him a financial gift through Epaphroditus, who traveled approximately 795 miles from Philippi to Rome to deliver their offering to Paul while he was in prison[1] (Phil. 2:25–29; Phil. 4:14–18).

After receiving their gift, Paul sent Epaphroditus, who almost died on the journey, back to the Philippian church with his thanks and the letter we now call the Epistle to the Philippians.

ACTS 15

Take a moment and read through Acts 15. This will give us the context for where Paul was in his ministry as he first headed into Philippi.

Acts 15 opens by describing how men (who are called Judaizers elsewhere in Scripture) were promoting the false teaching of salvation-through-circumcision. To our modern minds, this may not seem like a serious issue. However, Jewish believers in the early church were still struggling to accept that uncircumcised Gentiles could worship the One True God without following the customs and covenant God had set forth with Moses.

The issue was so contested that the apostles and elders held a council in Jerusalem to settle the matter. After much debate, the apostles concluded that since the Gentiles received the Holy Spirit when they believed the same way the Jewish believers had *while remaining uncircumcised*, it was evident that circumcision was not a necessary part of a person's salvation.

The apostles sent Paul and Barnabas back to Antioch, along with Silas and Judas, to assure the believers that circumcision was not a necessary step for salvation. The believers received the news with gladness, and Paul and Barnabas stayed with them for some time, teaching and encouraging them.

Things looked promising in Paul's ministry at this point. He was instrumental in defending the truth of the gospel from false teaching. He was in good favor with the other apostles in Jerusalem and was used to deliver their message to Antioch. God used him to minister in many ways, and he had his faithful companion Barnabas by his side.

Here's where the story turns.

Paul longed to visit the churches he and Barnabas had planted on their first missionary journey, and he asked Barnabas to go with him. Barnabas wanted to take John Mark along, but Paul didn't think that was a good idea because John Mark had deserted them on a previous trip. They both felt so strongly about their positions that they argued sharply and decided to go their separate ways!

These were two godly men who loved the gospel, were chosen and "set apart" by the Holy Spirit for the ministry (Acts 13:2), and had been sent out together on their first missionary journey. How could two such men allow a minor issue to divide them?

Undoubtedly, this split caused emotional pain for both Paul and Barnabas. They had traveled many places together, encouraging, supporting, and laboring side by side for the gospel.

DEAR MISSIONARY

Tomorrow on Day 1 of this devotional, you will study Acts 16, which details Paul's first visit to Philippi, but for today, let's reflect on what we can learn from Paul's split with Barnabas.

Was this split between these godly men God's will or the result of Satan's desire to cause conflict and division? The Bible doesn't tell us, but regardless of which it may be, we rest assured that God causes all things to work together for good (Rom. 8:28). Paul and Barnabas were both given over for God's purposes. God used their split to send the gospel into the world in two directions instead of one, thus effectively doubling their reach.

The split also caused Paul to take Silas and Timothy with him, strengthening and training them in the ministry, so that they also became passionate, effective evangelists.

DEAR MISSIONARY, if you serve in gospel ministry long enough, you will experience division, contention, and even splits between people you thought you would never see disagree. You might be in the middle of the split or find yourself and your ministry on the periphery of a conflict that hurts you.

Hold on to the hope that God is at work. He can bring good out of what seems hopeless. He will achieve His greater purposes.

Heed Paul's words in 1 Corinthians 15:58: "Therefore, my beloved brothers, be steadfast, immovable, always abounding in the work of the Lord, knowing that in the Lord, your labor is not in vain."

Even amid difficult circumstances, you are called to stand firm, abounding in the work of the Lord. In any situation, a missionary whose heart focuses on Christ will have perfect peace (Isa. 26:3).

Even amid turmoil, live the life of integrity God has called you to and walk humbly before your God (Mic. 6:8).

Paul and Barnabas reconciled later in their lives, and Paul spoke favorably of both Barnabas and John Mark (1 Cor. 9:6; 2 Tim. 4:11), even calling John Mark to his side because he was helpful in the ministry. What a beautiful demonstration of the unity of believers! Hold onto the hope that God can bring beauty even in challenging situations.

DEEP DIVE:

1) Use a dictionary to look up the word *steadfast*. What does it mean?

_____

_____

_____

_____

2) Read James 1:12. What does this verse say about the person who remains steadfast under trial?

_____

_____

_____

_____

3) Read Psalm 57:7. What does a steadfast heart do? Are you doing this amid your trials?

_____

_____

_____

_____

Day 1: Planting the Philippian Church

"Never be afraid to trust an unknown future to a known God."
~Corrie Ten Boom[1]

Read Acts 16.

In Acts 15 and 16, the gospel faced many setbacks. The false teaching of salvation-through-circumcision tried to derail the early church. An interpersonal conflict between the "dynamic duo" Paul and Barnabas seemed to spell disaster for the gospel's spread. Then, the Holy Spirit stopped Paul from evangelizing in Asia and Bithynia.

Just when Paul seemed to be making headway in Philippi, an evil spirit caused chaos, and the magistrates threw Paul into jail. Paul could have succumbed to discouragement, but instead, he responded by praying and singing hymns to God. He maintained his faith, trusting that God was actively achieving his purposes in every situation and working all things together for good.

How do we see God's faithfulness in this chapter?

Because Paul and Barnabas headed in different directions, the gospel's spread doubled. God provided Paul with two new ministry partners, Silas and young Timothy, who grew into a strong leader in the church.

When God directed Paul into Macedonia, and he preached in Philippi, he gained the first Christian converts on European soil, thus opening a new continent to the gospel.

Paul's encounter with the demon-possessed slave girl demonstrated God's power over the spiritual realm and gave credibility to Paul's gospel message. Then God directly used Paul's arrest, imprisonment, and the chain-breaking earthquake for the jailer's salvation.

In time, God healed the broken relationship between Paul and John Mark. Late in his life, Paul specifically called for John Mark to come to him because he was helpful to Paul for the ministry (2 Tim. 4:11).

DEAR MISSIONARY, we serve a mighty God. Nothing can stand against him. What setback are you facing today? What circumstances seem impossible to overcome? What roadblocks are hindering the gospel in your ministry?

Despite everything, follow Paul's example and worship. Your loving heavenly Father, who promised to work all things together for good (Rom. 8:28), is handling your situation. God sees your pain, and he knows your struggles. You can rest knowing that you do not have to find a solution. Your part is to trust him. "He has made everything beautiful in its time" (Eccles. 3:11).

DEEP DIVE:

1) Read Job 42:2. How does this strengthen your trust in God?

_____

_____

_____

_____

2) Read Psalm 57:2 and Psalm 138:8. How do these verses encourage you?

_____

_____

_____

_____

3) Reflect on your life. Looking back, how have you seen God work difficult circumstances together for your good and his glory?

_____

_____

_____

_____

Day 2: Joyful Surrender

"He is no fool who gives up what he cannot keep to gain that which he cannot lose."
~Jim Elliot, missionary to Ecuador[1]

Read Philippians 1:1–2.

Paul was not an ordinary man. He received the best education, studying under Gamaliel, the highly-esteemed Jewish rabbi, and progressed in Judaism faster than his peers. His sharp mind and strength of will are evident in his life and writings. God chose him for apostleship, gave him a vision of Jesus on the road to Damascus, and used him to perform miracles. Many people believed in the Lord Jesus through Paul's ministry.

As an apostle, evangelist, and church leader, he deserved

respect, yet, in Philippians 1:1, when Paul introduced himself to the Philippian church, he didn't mention any of his qualifications. Instead, he called himself a *bondservant* (NKJV) of Jesus Christ (some translations use *servant*). Translated literally, a bondservant is a slave (the Greek word *doulos*).

Under Mosaic Law, when an indentured slave fulfilled his duty to his master (often working to pay off a debt), he could volunteer to remain in service to his master. As evidence of his willingness to continue permanently under his master's authority, the master used an awl to drill a hole through the bondservant's ear into a doorpost (Exod. 21:1–6; Deut. 15:12–17).

Slavery under Roman law differed from slavery under the Mosaic Law, but it was prevalent in Paul's time and familiar to the Philippian church. Roman law gave a master complete authority over his slave, and he could kill the slave without repercussion. The slave was entirely at his master's disposal.

Drawing from both the Mosaic and Roman understanding of slavery, Paul referred to himself as a bondservant, demonstrating how he viewed his relationship with Jesus. Jesus was his Lord and master, and Paul was his bondservant, willingly and wholly given to Jesus' purposes.

Does God require any less of us today?

Matthew 16:24–25 says:

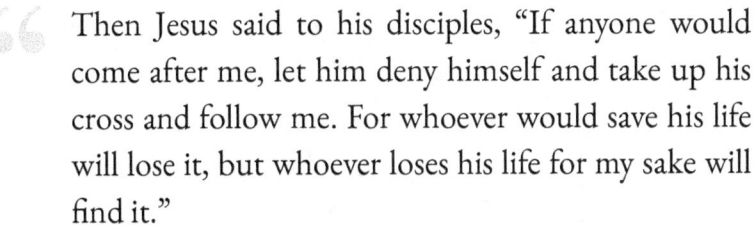

> Then Jesus said to his disciples, "If anyone would come after me, let him deny himself and take up his cross and follow me. For whoever would save his life will lose it, but whoever loses his life for my sake will find it."

Jesus' call to believers to deny themselves and follow him requires absolute surrender. Half-hearted surrender is not surrender at all.

Our modern understanding of slavery makes us bristle at the thought of being a slave to anyone, but being a bondservant to Jesus is not demeaning. Jesus does not abuse or degrade his followers. Jesus came that we may "have life and have it abundantly" (John 10:10). Jesus is the joy-giver, and surrender to him is the gateway to joy. You cannot find joy in any other way.

Absolute surrender is absolute joy.

Only when you lose your life by giving it to follow Jesus will you find the abundant life Christ promised you.

DEAR MISSIONARY, you have probably already settled this issue of surrender in your heart. You wouldn't have come as far as you have without giving Jesus authority over your life. Yet surrender is often hardest in the minor inconveniences, annoyances, and frustrating circumstances of life. At such times, it's easy to forget you must surrender every moment to the Lord. When you find yourself rebelling against what God—in his sovereignty—has allowed in your life, remember your identity as a bondservant of Christ. If you claim Jesus as Lord, you must submit your will to his. Then you become a living sacrifice (Rom. 12:2) and a pleasant aroma, useful for his work.

Are you lacking joy? Has the work God put before you become drudgery? You may need to surrender yourself again to the Lord. Consciously give him the right to do whatever he wants to with your life, and allow his joy to flood you afresh.

DEEP DIVE:

1) Read the opening verses of each of the epistles in the New Testament. How often do you see an author call himself a *servant* or *bondservant*? Who, other than Paul, referred to themselves in this way?

_____

_____

_____

_____

2) Read what Paul writes in 1 Corinthians 7:22, Ephesians 6:6, and 2 Timothy 2:24 about being a bondservant/servant. How does this challenge you to surrender to God? Prayerfully examine your life for any areas you might be withholding from the Lord.

_____

_____

_____

_____

3) In Philippians 1:1, Paul writes to the saints who are both "in Philippi" and "in Christ Jesus." How does this encourage you when you find your physical location on the mission field wearying?

_____

_____

_____

_____

Day 3: Christian Maturity

"Behold, how good and pleasant it is when brothers dwell in
unity!"
Psalm 133:1

Read Philippians 1:3–8 and Ephesians 4:1–16.

In Ephesians 4, Paul lays out two goals for the church: unity and
maturity. Christian unity is only possible because believers share
the same heavenly Father. Believers are "in Christ," members of
Christ's body (1 Cor. 12:27), and in-dwelt by the Holy Spirit. We
all partake of the same grace (Phil. 1:7).

Unity is possible through Jesus Christ but does not come
automatically, so Paul encourages believers to be "eager to maintain the unity of the Spirit in the bond of peace" (Eph. 4:3).

In the following verses, Paul explains how unity and maturity are achieved. Church leaders—apostles, prophets, evangelists, shepherds (pastors), and teachers—have two jobs: equipping the saints for ministry and building up the body of Christ.

When leaders are faithful in these tasks, believers grow in their knowledge of Jesus, mature in their faith, walk in unity, and grow in the fullness of Christ.

A church that has matured in these ways will not be deceived by false doctrines, "human cunning," and "craftiness in deceitful schemes" (Eph. 4:14).

Paul's relationship with the Philippian church is a beautiful model of Ephesians 4 in action.

First, Paul lovingly instructed the Philippian believers in doctrine and labored for their sake, enduring hardship and imprisonment. In turn, the Philippians demonstrated their love for Paul through their prayers and financial support.

Their mutual, loving behavior produced the sweet fellowship detailed in Philippians 1:3–8. Paul—filled with thankfulness and joy—overflowed with affection for the Philippian believers, praying for them often. He held them in his heart and longed for them with the affection of Jesus Christ. In Philippians 4:1, he called them his joy and his crown.

Second, Paul's teaching helped the Philippians mature in their faith and avoid being deceived by Satan's lies. In most of Paul's epistles, he had to write at length to correct the false teachers who were deceiving the churches, but in his letter to the Philippians, he gave only one brief reminder that salvation is not through works of the flesh.

Third, Paul's faithful instruction equipped the Philippians for ministry, allowing him to rejoice in their "partnership in the gospel from the first day until now." They were not spectators but actively labored alongside Paul for the gospel (Phil. 4:3), united with him in their common goal.

In Philippians 1:9–11, Paul continued to seek their maturation as he prayed for their love to "abound more and more, with knowledge and all discernment" so they could "approve what is excellent" and be "pure and blameless" and "filled with the fruit of righteousness." The Philippians grew because of Paul's faithful work and prayers.

DEAR MISSIONARY, how do you spend your time and energy? Have you kept the unity and maturity of the church at the heart of your ministry activities? Are you equipping the saints for the work of the Lord through your faithful instruction and discipleship? Are you keeping "the knowledge of the Son of God" at the heart of your message to believers and non-believers alike? Are you promoting unity through humility, gentleness, patience, and love? (Eph. 4:2).

Consider and rejoice in your unique and blessed position in the body of Christ. You get to experience and promote the church's unity in two (or more) local fellowships—the one that sent you and the one you now minister to. You have partners back home who stand with you in prayer and financial support. In turn, you report on God's faithfulness and the growth of the global church. You also get to participate in church life in your host country, teaching and being taught by your new church family.

Your place in Christ's body spans cultures and continents, and you experience a little taste of heaven's unity, where people from every tribe, tongue, and nation stand together before God's throne and cry out, "Holy, holy, holy, is the Lord God almighty!" (Rev. 4:8).

DEEP DIVE:

1) Examine your ministry activities in light of Ephesians 4:1–16. Are you involved in a local church? Are your efforts building up the church "in Christ"? What changes can you make to your ministry or how you spend your time to better focus on helping others grow in their faith?

_____

_____

_____

_____

2) When you minister among the lost, how do you keep sharing the knowledge of the Son of God (Eph. 4:13) at the forefront?

_____

_____

_____

_____

3) How are you building the body of Christ in your sending church back home?

_____

_____

_____

_____

Day 4: The Promise of Completion

"If I have not the patience of my
Saviour with souls who grow
slowly;
if I know little of travail (a sharp
and painful thing) till Christ be
fully formed in them,
then I know nothing of Calvary love."
~ Amy Carmichael, missionary to India[1]

Read Philippians 1:3–8.

In Romans 7:15–25, Paul lamented his fleshly weaknesses. He did things he didn't like and failed to do what he should. He cried to be delivered from his "body of death."

We identify with Paul's struggle because we find the same recurring battle with sin in our lives. Yet even when we fail, we find hope in this: God is at work in every believer's life. He draws us to himself, convicts us of sin, calls us to repentance, and makes us new creations (2 Cor. 5:17).

Salvation is only the beginning. God then begins to sanctify us, conforming us to the image of his Son. God calls us to holiness (1 Pet. 1:15), but he doesn't ask us to do anything he doesn't equip and empower us to do.

2 Peter 1:3–4 says:

> His divine power has granted to us all things that pertain to life and godliness, through the knowledge of him who called us to his own glory and excellence, by which he has granted to us his precious and very great promises, so that through them you may become partakers of the divine nature, having escaped from the corruption that is in the world because of sinful desire.

What a beautiful promise! God gave us everything we need to live a holy life. Nothing is lacking. Through Christ, God provided a way to escape corruption and sinful desires. He sent us the Holy Spirit, who guides us into truth (John 16:13) and empowers us to turn away from sin and walk in righteousness.

When we fail, we choose to walk by the flesh instead of by the Spirit. Our sinful desires entice us. This is the problem Paul lamented in Romans 7. Our spirits are willing, but our flesh is weak.

God does not abandon us in our struggle. Paul wrote to the

believers in Philippians 1:6: "And I am sure of this, that he who began a good work in you will bring it to completion at the day of Jesus Christ."

God will continue the process of sanctification in a believer's life until the day Christ returns, and our "bodies of death" are transformed to be like his glorified body.

DEAR MISSIONARY, allow this promise to encourage you in your personal struggles but also take encouragement for the people you are ministering to. Discipleship is frustrating when you care more about a person's spiritual growth than they do. You may feel you labor in vain, but rest assured, God is at work in every true believer's heart. He began and will complete their sanctification. Take the pressure off yourself and trust God. He cares for their growth more than you do.

The same God "who is able to keep you from stumbling and to present you blameless before the presence of his glory with great joy" (Jude 24) will do the same for all his children.

DEEP DIVE:

1) Dig into 2 Peter 1:3–11. What do these verses teach you about sanctification?

_____

_____

_____

_____

2) Read 1 Corinthians 3:5–9. What is your role? What is God's role?

_____

_____

_____

_____

3) Read Romans 8:1–17. What is the Spirit called in verse 2? What does he do?

_____

_____

_____

_____

4) Read Matthew 11:28–30. How does an easy yoke and light burden relate to salvation and sanctification?

_____

_____

_____

_____

Day 5: A Prayer for Growth

"The history of missions is the history of answered prayer."
~Samuel Zwemer[1]

Read Philippians 1:9–11.

On Day 4, we examined Ephesians 4 and the need for church growth in unity and maturity. In Philippians 1:9–11, Paul prayed specifically for the Philippian believers in these same two areas.

In verse 9, he prayed that their "love may abound more and more." Love, as defined in 1 Corinthians 13, is patient and kind. Love is not selfish, envious, or boastful. Love endures all things and rejoices with the truth. Love summarizes all the Law: love God and love your neighbor as yourself (Luke 10:27).

Love is a fruit of the Holy Spirit (Gal. 5:22–23). In this way,

Paul's prayer was for the Philippians to walk by the Spirit and not by the flesh.

When each member of Christ's body functions properly and leads a Spirit-filled life, it "makes the body grow so that it builds itself up in love" (Eph. 4:16). Love builds and unifies the church despite its people having different cultures, ethnic backgrounds, and social positions.

But when love is replaced with sinful behavior like envy, gossip, slander, pride, bitterness, selfishness, and anger, the body destroys itself. In Paul's rebuke to the Galatians regarding their disagreements, he pointed out that if they continued to bite and devour one another, they would consume one another (Gal. 5:15).

Paul also prayed that the Philippians would mature in knowledge and discernment. Knowledge (information and facts) and discernment (distinguishing between good and evil) come from God's Word.

Scripture is truth and renews a person's mind, so that the believer can discern God's good, pleasing, and perfect will (Rom. 12:2). A discerning Christian can approve what is excellent in doctrine and deed. A believer well-versed in Scripture is not easily deceived and uses wisdom to recognize dangerous situations in life.

Paul also prayed the Philippians would be "pure and blameless" and "filled with the fruit of righteousness that comes through Jesus Christ." This is a prayer for godly behavior, as conformity to the image of Jesus is God's will for every believer (1 Thess. 4:3).

DEAR MISSIONARY, as a Christian, prayer is your weapon. Paul's prayer gives us a solid model to follow when praying for ourselves and the people we minister to. Love, discernment, and holiness cover much of what is necessary for Christian maturity.

Paul's prayer is also helpful in evaluating your spiritual life. Are you actively building up the body of Christ and promoting unity through love? Are you consistently sharpening your knowledge and discernment through studying God's Word? Have you kept watch over your heart? Or have you allowed yourself to compromise on issues of righteousness?

Without honest self-assessment, you are unlikely to grow as a believer. But if you allow the Holy Spirit to show you your weaknesses, and you take them to the Lord in prayer, he promises to help you overcome them.

Your maturity is his delight.

DEEP DIVE:

1) Compare Philippians 1:9–11 with Romans 12:1–2. How are they in agreement?

_____

_____

_____

_____

2) Read Ephesians 4 and 5, and note Paul's directions regarding pure living and godly behavior. Why must we "walk in love" (Eph. 5:2)?

_____

_____

_____

_____

3) Read Titus 2:1–15. List all the attitudes and behaviors of a mature believer mentioned in these verses.

_____

_____

_____

_____

Day 6: God's Purposes are Never Thwarted

❧❀❧

"Let God have your life; He can do more with it than you can."
~Dwight L. Moody[1]

Read Philippians 1:12–14.

Paul wrote this epistle from prison and wanted to use his situation to teach the Philippians a vital truth: God is always in control, and nothing thwarts his plans.

From a human perspective, Paul's arrest and imprisonment looked like a disaster. Ancient prisons were places of suffering, hardship, disease, and death, and the Philippians feared for Paul's health and safety. He had done nothing wrong, and his restricted movement hindered him from spreading the gospel (they thought).

Why would the God who had commanded Paul to preach the gospel allow him to be arrested?

A lesser man would have filled his letter with pleas for help, accusations against his captors, complaints about his circumstances, and doubts about God's sovereignty and goodness. But instead of whining, Paul looked beyond the bleakness of his surroundings and recognized his imprisonment benefitted the advancement of the gospel (v. 12).

In verse 13, Paul explained how his situation had become "known throughout the whole imperial guard and to all the rest." The guards, the servants, the slaves, and the government officials heard the name of Jesus because of Paul. Paul's imprisonment gave him access to the ears of influential people. His guards rotated, giving him a fresh audience every day. Due in part to Paul and his chains, the gospel penetrated the heart of the Roman Empire.

When Paul evaluated his situation, he chose to focus on advancing the kingdom of God. He set his mind on heavenly things, not earthly things (Col. 3:2). He kept an eternal perspective in circumstances designed to cause despair. Paul rejoiced in his imprisonment because he recognized God was using it to propel the gospel forward.

In verse 13, Paul stated, "My chains are in Christ." He recognized God had allowed his arrest, and if God wanted him free, even the thickest physical chain could not hold him. Paul had experienced miraculous prison breaks before (Acts 16), and he knew God could break him free again if he chose. Chains did not hold Paul in prison; Christ did. God was achieving his greater purposes through Paul's chains, which even the non-believers around him recognized.

DEAR MISSIONARY, what hardship are you enduring right now? What is God accomplishing through the trials in your life?

Recognizing God's hand is difficult in the midst of a trial. Bleak situations seem unredeemable, and human reason cannot find a solution. Trust him. Your trial may be for your sanctification, or it might be the very thing God uses to advance the gospel in your mission field. Resolve to be a "living sacrifice" and allow God to do what he knows is best.

Recognize that, like Paul, your "chains" are in Christ. Keep an eternal perspective, focus on Jesus, and allow God to glorify himself in your situation and body, whether by life or death (Phil 1:20).

Surrender. God is at work.

DEEP DIVE:

1) Read Luke 21:12. How do you see this fulfilled in Paul's life?

_____

_____

_____

_____

2) Compare the life of Joseph (Genesis 37–46; 50) with the life of Paul. How is Joseph's statement in Genesis 45:4–8 reflected in Paul's life?

_____

_____

_____

_____

3) Compare the story of Esther with Paul's story. How does Mordecai's evaluation of Esther's purpose in Esther 4:14 align with the purpose Paul sees for himself?

_____

_____

_____

_____

4) How does this encourage you in your current challenges?

_____

_____

_____

_____

Day 7: Rivalry on the Mission Field

꧁❀꧂

"It is possible my life will be spared; if so, with what [zeal] shall I pursue my work! If not—His will be done. The door will be open for others who will do the work better."
~Adoniram Judson, missionary to Burma[1]

Read Philippians 1:12–18.

As noted in verse 14, Paul's chains galvanized the Christian brothers around him, and many of them began to evangelize boldly. Some saw Paul's restrictions and, moved by love, eagerly stepped into the gap to share the gospel.

However, some of the brothers were motivated to preach because of "envy," "rivalry," "selfish ambition," and the desire to "add affliction" to Paul's chains.

These conniving men may have been jealous of Paul's apostleship or his effectiveness in proclaiming truth and planting churches. Perhaps they were envious that God had used him to perform miracles, or they may have seen Paul's imprisonment as a golden opportunity to seize his ministry and position in the church for their own gain.

Paul doesn't tell us precisely what these men did (which is a sign of his maturity). However, none of these possibilities are farfetched. Sadly, missionaries do the same things today.

Pride is the root cause of most conflicts within the missionary community. Destructive and insidious, pride hides deep in the human heart. If a Christian does not fight against his pride and cling to the Savior, he will be overtaken.

Pride lures us into the comparison trap, where we measure our budgets, converts, spiritual gifts, and the difficulty of our mission field against those of other missionaries. These comparisons happen so subtly that you may not even realize you are being ensnared. When people compare themselves, nobody wins. If you think you are better than your brother, your heart fills with pride. If you feel you are worse, your heart fills with jealousy. Either way, you sin, and your sin comes between you and your brother.

Pride also tempts us to exploit another missionary's weaknesses to make our own strengths look good. It's easy to show off to gain respect from others while hiding personal flaws and sins.

Instead of cooperating, missionaries sometimes compete. Leaders may vie for power and demand things be done their way; teams split, damaging the ministry and wounding individuals with harsh words and unloving behavior. Unrepentance, unforgiveness, and lack of reconciliation allow pride to wreak havoc on the lives of missionaries and their ministries.

DEAR MISSIONARY, have you experienced competition on the mission field? Have you fallen into the comparison trap? Have you been wounded by a team member or missionary from another organization?

Paul's response to these envious men, who wanted to kick him while he was down, instructs us about handling our interpersonal conflicts.

When Paul and Barnabas quarreled over John Mark at the end of Acts 15, both demanded their own way, refused to cooperate, and decided to split.

Ten years later, Paul responded to these envious men with a grace and forbearance he had not shown to Barnabas and John Mark. Instead of protesting their ill-treatment and getting angry over their wrong motives, Paul chose to rejoice that Christ was being preached.

The cross is the singular focus we must keep at all times. You may disagree with another missionary's methods, you may see their weaknesses, and they may have hurt you in the past, but fix your eyes on the cross. God will deal with their issues in his own time.*

Paul continued to call these men "brothers," willingly forgiving the wrongs done against him. Remember that he reconciled with Barnabas and John Mark and was eager to work with him in the ministry (2 Tim. 4:11).

When you face conflict on the mission field with team members or Christians from other ministries, follow the example of the older-and-wiser Paul and be a peacemaker (Matt. 5:7), ready to forgive. Don't view another's success or spiritual gifts as a threat. Instead, rejoice that Christ is being preached.

Don't look to the left or the right. Instead, faithfully do what God has called you to, keep your heart right before the Lord, and entrust everything else to him.

DEEP DIVE:

1) Read James 3:13–18. Examine the cause-and-effect relationships of heavenly wisdom, envy, and selfishness.

_____

_____

_____

_____

2) Read Romans 12:18. How do you need to apply this verse in your life today?

_____

_____

_____

_____

3) Read Romans 14:1–4. How can verse 4 apply to the issue of pride and jealousy on the mission field?

_____

_____

_____

_____

*I am not suggesting that issues should never be confronted. The Bible teaches that "iron sharpens iron" (Prov. 27:17), and we are to lovingly correct, rebuke, and seek forgiveness when we wrong each other (Matthew 5:21–26 and Matthew 18:15–20). The point I am making here is that it is not your job to seek revenge or try to force someone to change. Only the Holy Spirit can bring true conviction that leads to repentance.

Day 8: Attitude of Triumph

"It is remarkable that in all his writings Paul's prayers for his friends contain no appeals for changes in their circumstances."
~Charles Spurgeon[1]

Read Philippians 1:19–26.

Today's verses contain one of the most well-known passages in Paul's writing, where he cried out: "For to me to live is Christ, and to die is gain" (v. 21). This is a simple but profound encapsulation of the Christian life.

When Paul penned those words, the outcome of his imprisonment was uncertain. Yet, in verse 19, he stated with confidence that the Philippians' prayers on his behalf were accomplishing what they intended—his deliverance.

The Philippians, concerned with Paul's physical well-being, were praying for his deliverance from his chains, but Paul didn't limit deliverance to physical freedom. He declared that it didn't matter what happened to him because his ultimate goal of magnifying Christ in his body could be accomplished in either life or death.

To magnify something is to make it prominent and visible. The goal of the Christian life is to make Christ "visible" to everyone.

Paul realized that if he died, Christ would be magnified by Paul's willingness to stand firm in the faith, unwavering in the face of death. Having kept his testimony to the end, Paul would set an example for all the believers and declare to every spectator that Christ was worth dying for. Paul even longed for this, knowing death meant deliverance from the struggles of a sin-sick world and entrance into heaven.

Paul didn't view death as defeat. He felt no shame over his chains. Instead, he considered his imprisonment and the possibility of death as a triumph. What could death do to him except set him free and usher him into God's presence?

Paul's only regret was that if he died, he would no longer be able to help the Philippians and the other believers in their faith. He longed to labor for their sake, and at the end of this passage in verses 24–26, Paul concluded that he would continue living for the benefit of the Philippians' spiritual growth. If he lived and continued his ministry, Christ would be magnified in his life.

DEAR MISSIONARY, we have come again to this issue of surrender. First, you must surrender to your purpose: magnifying Christ in your body. In 1 Corinthians 6:20, Paul admonished the believers that their lives and bodies no longer belonged to them because they had been bought with a price—Christ's blood. We must rise every morning with our God-glorifying purpose at the forefront of our minds.

Second, you must surrender to God's method for magnifying Christ in your life. What opportunity for dying to self and glorifying the name of Jesus has God laid before you?

You may face death, tropical diseases, or reoccurring illnesses that leave you weak and longing for the comforts of home. Or your opportunity to magnify Christ in your body might be in the unrelenting challenges of parenthood and homemaking in a demanding environment where you can't keep up with the work. Perhaps your gift to Christ is in your faithful Bible translation for an uncooperative, unfriendly, unappreciative people group. Your chance to magnify Christ may look like a problematic church member who doesn't seem to mature, no matter how much counsel you provide.

Remaining steadfast requires you to remember you are a bondservant in the loving hands of our glorious God. Follow him in wholehearted obedience in whatever situation you face, and allow Christ to magnify himself in you.

DEEP DIVE:

1) Read 1 Corinthians 15:55. What is Paul's evaluation of the power of death?

_____

_____

_____

_____

2) Analyze 1 Corinthians 6:19–20. What is Paul's argument for why we must live a holy life?

_____

_____

_____

_____

3) Reread Philippians 1:19. What two factors does Paul declare are working together for his deliverance?

_____

_____

_____

4) Why are both factors necessary?

_____

_____

_____

Day 9: Citizen of Heaven

"If you are a Christian, you are not a citizen of this world trying to
get to heaven; you are a citizen of heaven making your way
through this world."
~Vance Havner[1]

Read Philippians 1:27–30.

Though Paul felt confident he would see the Philippians again, he
did not know if or when God would allow him to return, so he
admonished the Philippians to conduct themselves in a manner
worthy of the gospel.

In verse 27, the word translated into English as "conduct"
(NKJV/NIV) or "manner" (ESV) has the same root as the English

word for "politics." Translated literally, it means "to live as a citizen."

In Philippians 3:20, Paul more fully explained this when he said: "Our citizenship is in heaven." In short, Paul told the Philippians, "You belong to heaven, so act like it. Behave as a citizen of heaven would behave!"

Just as ambassadors represent their sending-government, believers represent Christ to the world. God requires us to live as citizens of heaven, even though we are not there yet. We must have the attitudes and behaviors of someone who dwells in God's presence.

Paul also admonished the Philippians to live faithful, holy lives whether he was physically with them or not. He did not want them to behave one way while he was with them and another when he was away. The Christian life must be lived in integrity.

DEAR MISSIONARY, we cannot take personal integrity seriously enough. A hypocritical life is deadly to a missionary's testimony and can do more to destroy a ministry than almost everything else. We must strive to honor Christ in every action, whether seen by men or only by God.

Paul called the Philippians to consistent, God-honoring behavior because he knew the temptation of living to be seen and praised by men. Ministry can become a performance where we display only what we want others to see. Our mission fields are often far away from those we report to; they will know only what we tell them. Does your missionary newsletter document the truth of what is happening with your ministry? Are your financial statements accurate? Are you a different person when short-term teams from your sending-church visit than when you are alone? Are you a different person as a husband or wife in private than in public?

There will be no deceit in heaven. Nor will there be any pride or self-seeking behavior. We must leave no room for these things in our lives here and now.

On a side note, the idea of heavenly citizenship may be useful for helping new believers decide which parts of their culture are acceptable for them to continue participating in and which are not. Consider each behavior, and ask if it is appropriate for someone whose citizenship is in heaven.

For example, would a citizen of heaven practice witchcraft? No! Would a citizen of heaven brew traditional alcohol, knowing it leads to drunkenness in the community? No!

Would a citizen of heaven negotiate for land, livestock, or a wife in the same way as his forefathers? Maybe. Maybe not. The answer will depend on the details of the situation, but evaluating the behavior's appropriateness for someone whose true citizenship is in heaven may help someone discern what will honor God.

DEEP DIVE:

1) Study the use of the word "integrity" in Scripture. Genesis 20:5, Psalm 7:8, and Proverbs 19:1 will get you started. What do these verses teach you about integrity?

_____

_____

_____

_____

2) Read Colossians 3:23. What antidote do these verses give to the temptation to be seen and praised by men? Evaluate your behavior as a missionary according to this standard.

_____

_____

_____

_____

3) How should being a citizen of heaven change your desires, thoughts, and attitudes? Reference Colossians 1:9–14, Colossians 3:2, and Philippians 2:21.

_____

_____

_____

_____

Day 10: Stand Firm Without Fear

"We shouldn't pray for a lighter load to carry but a stronger back
to endure! Then the world will see that God is with us,
empowering us to live in a way that reflects his love and power."
~Brother Yun[1]

Read Philippians 1:27–30.

In verse 27, Paul told the Philippians to honor Christ with their
behavior. He then used two metaphors to explain what that
behavior should look like.

"Stand firm" refers to a soldier standing his ground on the
battlefield, undaunted by his enemies. "Striving side by side" refers
to a sports team working in unity to win a competition. Taken
together, the Philippians were to stand shoulder to shoulder as

brave soldiers with their shields locked together, working as a unified team to defend the gospel.

In verse 28, Paul explained that they must contend for the faith without fear so that it would testify to their adversaries that they were headed for destruction because they opposed God (Acts 5:38–39). They would also realize they lacked the supernatural power the Christians possessed.

To a believer, his boldness was proof that his salvation and relationship with God were genuine because the Holy Spirit empowered him. One of the outcomes of the Holy Spirit's presence in the apostles' lives on the day of Pentecost was their sudden boldness in evangelism (Acts 4:13). Who else but a mighty God could take a trembling group of men and transform them into courageous evangelists? When a Christian is fearless and stands firm beyond what is humanly possible, it is evidence of the great God whom the Christian trusts. The unyielding, warrior spirit of the Christian who boldly proclaims truth—even to the point of death—is the loudest testimony to the world of the marvelous God he serves.

DEAR MISSIONARY, we do not often consider our boldness to be a witnessing tool, but Paul said it demonstrates both salvation and damnation to those who witness it. Instead of utilizing the powerful testimony of bold faith, it's tempting to look for an easy way out at the first sign of trouble. When threatened with violence, some choose to compromise the Word of God to avoid strife. Even within the church, we hesitate to confront sin because we want to sidestep conflict and please men more than we want to please God.

We may not realize it, but such behaviors come from fear and demonstrate the weakness of our conviction.

Jude 20 instructs us to build ourselves up in the faith, and we do so by knowing God's unfailing character and his Word. The American evangelist Dwight L. Moody said, "When we find a man meditating on the words of God, my friends, that man is full of boldness and is successful."[2]

Take heart. God's promises are true, and he will strengthen you for the day of battle. Take time to meditate on these truths and build yourself up in God's Word:

- If God is for you, who can be against you (Rom. 8:31–32)?
- He will never leave you nor forsake you (Deut. 31:8) and is with you to the end of the age (Matt. 28:20).
- The Lord has not given you a spirit of fear (2 Tim. 1:7–8).
- "He who is in you is greater than he who is in the world" (1 John 4:4).
- He holds you in his righteous right hand (Isa. 41:10).
- In all things, you are more than conquerors (Rom. 8:37).
- His divine power has given you everything you need for life and godliness (2 Pet. 1:3).
- The righteous are bold as a lion (Prov. 28:1).
- Put on the armor of God so you can stand (Eph. 6:10–20).

DEEP DIVE:

1) Read Acts 4. What astonished the Jewish leaders in verse 13? What did the apostles pray for in verses 29–30?

_____

_____

_____

_____

2) Read Acts 5:17–42. What wisdom did Gamaliel show as he evaluated the situation described in these verses?

_____

_____

_____

_____

3) How does this fit with Philippians 1:28?

_____

_____

_____

_____

4) Read Ephesians 6:18–20. After telling us how to stand firm in the armor of God, what did Paul request the believers to pray for him about?

_____

_____

_____

_____

5) Read David's speech to Goliath in 1 Samuel 17:45–47. Whose name did he use as he approached Goliath? What would David's victory demonstrate to all the earth? What lessons on boldness do you draw from David's story?

_____

_____

_____

_____

Day 11: The Gift of Suffering

"The term 'passion' is used to describe everything from romance
to hunger pangs. I don't know what it means to you, but for me
passion means whatever a person is willing to suffer for. In fact,
that's the root meaning of the word. It comes from the Latin
paserre, to suffer. It is what you hunger for so intensely that you
will sacrifice anything to have it."
~Floyd McClung[1]

Read Philippians 1:27–30.

In verse 28, Paul admonished the Philippians to stand firm in their
faith without fear of those who opposed them and the gospel. In
verse 29, Paul identified what they feared: suffering. Suffering

comes in many forms: poverty, famine, diseases, war, persecution, imprisonment, and torture, to name just a few.

It's natural to want to avoid these things, but in verse 29, Paul flipped the issue of suffering on its head. Instead of treating suffering as something to be mitigated at all costs, Paul elevated it.

The word translated into English as "granted" in verse 29 is from the same word as "grace." Suffering for Christ is a privilege and gift given through grace, just like salvation.[2]

We usually think of God's grace as the source of the positive things in our lives, like financial success, good health, and other blessings, while blaming trials and persecution on Satan or the result of living in a fallen world.

We celebrate the gift of Jesus' sacrifice on our behalf as the ultimate form of grace while simultaneously running from and rejecting our own suffering. When we suffer, we are tempted to point our finger at God and ask him how he could allow pain in our lives. We question his goodness and sovereignty over the world. Consider Job's words to his wife in the face of his suffering, "Shall we receive good from the Lord and shall we not receive evil?" (Job 2:10).

In Philippians 3:10, Paul explained that suffering on behalf of Christ is fellowship with him. Through the fellowship of suffering, the believer knows Christ more and becomes more like him. If we never experienced suffering as Christ did, there would be an aspect of Christ we could not understand, and the reality of his sacrifice on our behalf would appear dull and inconsequential. But because we also suffer, we greatly appreciate the price Christ paid for our salvation.

In James 1:2–4, James explained that suffering is beneficial because persevering through trials produces character and makes the believer "perfect" and "complete." In Matthew 5:10–12, during the sermon on the mount, Jesus promised those who suffer for righteousness that the kingdom of heaven belongs to them and their reward in heaven will be great.

In Acts 5, the apostles were arrested and stood trial before the Jewish Council, who threatened them with death, beat them, and then let them go. At the end of their ordeal, the apostles went away rejoicing they were counted worthy to suffer for Jesus' name (Acts 5:41).

DEAR MISSIONARY, it's one thing to realize that suffering for Jesus is a gift of grace, but how can you face suffering with a victorious attitude? Paul's counsel on this issue is laced throughout Philippians. We will take each verse in depth when we reach it, but for now, consider the list below and how it instructs your perspective on suffering.

1. Godly discernment helps you think rightly about suffering and endure while remaining pure and blameless (Phil. 1:10).
2. Remember that whether you live or die (are released from the suffering or must persevere), you are victorious in Christ (Phil. 1:21).
3. Remember that your boldness and patient endurance in suffering is a testimony of your salvation and your enemies' destruction (Phil. 1:28).
4. Remember your suffering is a privilege given through grace (Phil. 1:29).
5. Imitate Christ in his humility and obedience to God's will (Phil. 2:5–8).
6. Remember God is working his will in you (Phil. 2:13).

7. Endure without complaining to shine as a light in a dark world (Phil. 2:14).

8. Consider everything a loss compared to knowing Christ, being found in him, knowing his power, and the fellowship of suffering (Phil. 3:7–10).

9. Press on toward the goal of a mature Christian life, which is only achieved through perseverance (Phil. 3:12–14).

10. Focus on heavenly things and your citizenship in heaven (Phil. 3:20).

11. Rejoice in the Lord and pray with thanksgiving, and God's peace will guard your mind (Phil. 4:4–7).

12. Control your thoughts (Phil. 4:8).

13. Christ will give you the strength to be content in all circumstances (Phil. 4:11–13).

Which of these is the most difficult for you to implement? Which encourages you the most?

DEEP DIVE:

1) Read James 1:1–12. What reward is given to those who endure?

_____

_____

_____

_____

2) Read 2 Thessalonians 1:3–12. What parallels do you see between these verses and Philippians 1:28–30?

_____

_____

_____

_____

3) Read 2 Corinthians 4:8–18. What does suffering achieve according to these verses? (List at least 3.)

_____

_____

_____

_____

Day 12: Mind of Christ

"No man has the mind of Christ, except him who makes it his business to obey him."
~George MacDonald[1]

Read Philippians 2:1–11.

Paul closed Philippians Chapter One with instructions on standing against attacks from unbelievers. He opened Chapter Two by teaching the believers how to promote unity among themselves. Paul's approach was simple: each believer must have the mind of Christ, following his example in attitude, thought, and action.

Paul's first command in verse one is for believers to encourage one another. He was not referring to hollow platitudes like "You can do it!" or "Keep trying!" which lack substance and point a person toward their own strength. Genuine Christian encouragement must be based on everything a believer possesses "in Christ," like a new nature, new position, and the presence and power of the Holy Spirit. It must remind a believer to draw his strength from Jesus.

Paul also instructed believers to demonstrate the mind of Christ by loving and comforting each other with affection and compassion. These behaviors, which include having patience with each other's weaknesses (Col. 3:12–14), offering forgiveness, and not causing each other to stumble (1 Cor. 8:9), are evidence of the fruit of the Spirit in a believer's life.

Paul then contrasted a Christ-like, humble attitude with the sins of pride and selfish ambition. Pride is at work when believers refuse to submit to one another, are impatient, demanding, or refuse to be corrected. Selfish ambition prompts a person to promote himself at another's expense.

Humility is the antidote to both selfishness and pride. It leads a believer to respect others as being more important and to look to their interests by putting their needs and desires above one's own. This requires self-sacrifice.

Jesus demonstrated humility in both ways. He looked at humanity's desperate need for a Savior, put our well-being above his glory, humbled himself, and became a bondservant. Even when despised and rejected by men, he did not defend himself but went as a willing sacrifice to the cross.

DEAR MISSIONARY, you can apply these verses to yourself by asking one question: Where do my thoughts, attitudes, and will differ from Christ's?

The areas of your life where you follow Christ's example will be characterized by humility, thus promoting unity and producing joy. In the areas where you have not surrendered to Christ, pride and selfish ambition will still be at work, oozing toxic sin into your relationships.

Think of a relationship that brings you joy and another that causes you irritation. It will not take long for you to identify where Christ's character is lacking in the difficult relationship (either on your side or theirs), as sin will be present. Likewise, you will quickly recognize that Christ's love, peace, and kindness characterize your joyful relationships.

In our relationships with unbelievers, we must remember that they do not have the mind of Christ because they do not know Jesus. We, who are in Christ, must take the lead and demonstrate Christ-like love, patience, and forgiveness, thus displaying the Savior's beauty. Just as his *kindness* leads us to repentance (Rom. 2:4), and "we love because he first *loved* us" (1 John 4:19, emphasis added), we will draw others to Christ when we display the heart and mind of Christ in our lives.

DEEP DIVE:

1) Read Philippians 2:5–11. What did God do for Jesus after he humbled himself and died on the cross?

_____

_____

_____

_____

2) How does 1 Peter 4:5 relate to this?

_____

_____

_____

_____

3) Read Proverbs 10:12 and 1 Peter 4:8. How can you apply these verses in a difficult relationship today?

_____

_____

_____

_____

4) Start a list of verses that can be used as genuine Christian encouragement. For example, "The Lord is my shield" (Ps. 3:3) can be used to encourage a fearful believer. Continue adding to the list as you come across different verses in Scripture. Use these verses when you encourage other believers instead of offering empty words.

_____

_____

_____

_____

Day 13: Every Knee Will Bow

"Missions is not the ultimate goal of the church. Worship is.
Missions exists because worship doesn't."
~John Piper[1]

Read Philippians 2:5–11.

William Carey, known as the father of modern missions, served in India, where he buried two wives and three children. He struggled with his health and labored for seven years before seeing anyone come to Christ. What gave him the strength to serve, without furlough, for a total of forty-one years?

Jim Eliott and his colleagues were brutally murdered by the Huaorani (Auca) Indians of Ecuador. What prompted his widow,

Elisabeth Elliot, to take their young daughter and return as a missionary to the very people who killed her husband?

What has kept thousands of other missionaries on the field through wars, famine, persecution, and the threat of death? What keeps you on the mission field and encourages you when your labor for the Lord seems in vain? What fortifies you when the darkness surrounding you seems insurmountable?

Taking the good news of Jesus Christ to all the world is a monumental task and may seem impossible. We speak, but people reject the message. We offer hope, but people remain enslaved to religion, witchcraft, and Satan's lies. Those who do believe mature slowly, falling back into old habits and sinful patterns. The work is more than we can handle, and much of the church is indifferent about taking the gospel to the lost.

Despair, discouragement, and depression are real challenges missionaries face. At this very moment, you may be questioning your ability to fulfill the work God has put before you. You may feel like hanging your head or crawling back into bed and giving up, but instead of surrendering to your hopelessness, look up!

Your help comes from the Lord, the maker of heaven and earth (Ps.121:2). God is with you; the battle belongs to him (Prov. 21:31), and he gave us a sneak peek at the outcome (God wins). Someday, willing or not, every knee will bow, and every tongue will acknowledge that Jesus is Lord.

Your neighbor who clings to idols of wood or stone will recognize Christ's kingship. Your persecutors who gloat over the pain they cause you will realize they have been fighting against Christ himself. The eyes of the religious zealot who debated his Scripture against yours will be opened, and his arguments will crumble around him. The powerful government that sought to suppress God's Word will submit to God's sovereignty. Every argument and pretense that sets itself up against the knowledge of God will be destroyed (2 Cor. 10:5). Nothing will stand against the Lord.

God, who calls all peoples to himself, will be known among the nations. Revelation 7:9 paints the breathtaking picture of a scene from heaven where people from every tribe, tongue, and nation stand before his throne, crying out in worship to him. Take time today to savor the beauty of the Creator surrounded by his people, the sheep of his pasture (Ps. 100:3).

DEAR MISSIONARY, let this glimpse of heaven strengthen your hands for your tasks. The road ahead of you may appear long and the goal unachievable, but God deserves to be worshipped, and bringing glory to his name is worth every sacrifice.

Consider this quotation from Robert C. Shannon: "Never pity missionaries; envy them. They are where the real action is, where life and death, sin and grace, Heaven and Hell converge."[2]

Nate Saint, Jim Elliot's colleague, who also lost his life to the Huaorani Indians of Ecuador, wrote:

> "People who do not know the Lord ask why in the world we waste our lives as missionaries. They forget that they too are expending their lives ... and when the bubble has burst, they will have nothing of eternal significance to show for the years they have wasted."[3]

Is there anything else worth giving your life for? God's work is of eternal value. It's a *privilege* to give your life to see God's name glorified around the world.

DEEP DIVE:

1) Read Isaiah 45. In what ways does God declare himself sovereign?

_____

_____

_____

_____

2) What does God declare will happen in verses 21–23?

_____

_____

_____

_____

3) Read Galatians 6:9. Have you grown weary in doing good and given up on some aspect of your ministry?

_____

_____

_____

_____

4) Is there an area you have been neglecting that you can return to?

_____

_____

_____

_____

5) We need to keep the Lord Jesus as the focal point of our lives. We lose sight of him when we look too much at the world. Spend time today in prayerful worship and center your heart back on him.

_____

_____

_____

_____

Day 14: His Will

"O, that I could consecrate myself, soul and body, to his service
forever; O, that I could give myself up to him, so as never more to
attempt to be my own or to have any will or affection improper for
those conformed to him."
~Lottie Moon, missionary to China[1]

Read Philippians 2:12–13.

In this beautiful passage about Christ, Paul pointed to Jesus'
obedience as an example for us. Since Christ obeyed the Father,
even to the point of death, we also must obey God in everything.

Paul linked obedience with salvation when he wrote in verse
12: "Work out your own salvation with fear and trembling." This
does not mean you can earn your salvation through works. Scrip-

ture teaches salvation is a gift from God, through faith, and not of works (Eph. 2:8–9; Rom. 3:21–24).

Paul intended for believers to examine their lives for evidence they were truly converted. Paul told the church in Corinth: "Examine yourselves, to see whether you are in the faith. Test yourselves" (2 Cor. 13:5).

Jesus explained how to identify false teachers when he said, "You will recognize them by their fruits" (Matt. 7:16). A false teacher or false convert will not bear fruit that glorifies God. In contrast, a true believer's faith will be evident, especially in his obedience to God's Word.

Paul expected Christians to examine themselves for evidence of salvation with "fear and trembling," not with a flippant attitude. God is serious about holiness; when a believer recognizes his sin, he must eradicate it. Jesus left no room for excuses when he said an eye or hand that causes sin should be cut off (Matt. 18:8–9). Jesus was not instructing us to mutilate our bodies but to go to war with the sin we find in our lives and hearts.

Believers are responsible for turning from sin and pursuing righteousness, but our obedience works in tandem with the Holy Spirit's influence in our lives. Paul first commented on this in Philippians 1:5, when he assured the Philippians God would complete the work he began in their lives. In verse 13, he explained that God works in us "both to will and to work for his good pleasure."

God's will for every Christian is that they are conformed to the image of Jesus. This necessitates a change in every aspect of a person's being. When we are born again, we instantly receive a new nature, but changing our wills to match his is a process that God takes great pleasure in undertaking.

Psalm 37:4 says, "Delight yourself in the Lord, and he will give you the desires of your heart." In our selfishness, we use this verse as proof that God will satisfy our greed for riches, fame, or success. But the interpretation is quite different when we read this verse in light of Philippians 2:13. When a believer delights (finds joy and satisfaction) in God, God puts righteous desires into the believer's heart, changing his love for sin into a love of righteousness.

In short, God gives us both the desire and the ability to obey.

DEAR MISSIONARY, if you examine your life, you will recognize that God took your indifferent heart and filled it with a desire to see the gospel reach the nations. Your heart now burns with the same passion as God's. This happens to any believer willing to surrender to God because the great commission is for every person who follows Jesus (Matt. 28:18–20). He gave you the desire and the ability to "go into all the world."

Continue to surrender. Allow God to align your heart with his, and then obey, faithfully doing what God has put in front of you today. Don't get overwhelmed with finding God's will for your life. A. W. Tozer said: "The man or woman who is wholly or joyously surrendered to Christ can't make a wrong choice–any choice will be the right one."[2]

Continue to delight in the Lord, and He will direct your steps (Prov. 16:9).

DEEP DIVE:

1) Read Proverbs 3:5–6, Proverbs 16:9, and Psalm 37:4. What do they teach you about God's guidance in your life?
Read James 2:14–26. What point is James making about faith and good deeds?

_____

_____

_____

_____

2) Consider this quotation from Charles Spurgeon: "When your will is God's will, you will have your will."[3] In your own words, explain his point.

_____

_____

_____

_____

3) Have you found this to be true in your own life?

_____

_____

_____

_____

Day 15: Shine

"Be a good witness by the way you live. The way we live is often
more convincing than the words we say."
~Billy Graham[1]

Read Philippians 2:12–18.

Verses 14–16 continue Paul's instructions about obedience, which
he started in verse 12. God gives believers the will and the power to
obey (v. 13), but this obedience must be without grumbling (complaining) or disputing (arguing).

To complain is to fight against God, who, in his sovereignty,
orchestrates the circumstances of a person's life. Complaining
says, "My will is better than God's will" and "I need to let God
know he is making a mistake." Complaining, which is often

bursting with emotion, is rooted in pride and discontent and loudly protests what it perceives as unfair, unjust, or undeserved treatment.

Disputing (arguing) is an intellectual form of rejecting God's will, saying to him, "Why me? Why now? Your will doesn't make sense. If I had control over my life, everything would be better."

A grumbling, arguing believer displays the same rebellion against God as unbelievers in a "crooked and twisted generation." Grumbling and arguing often lead to graver sins.

But believers are called to be different, accepting God's sovereignty and obeying Him in all circumstances with a submitted heart. When Christians live blameless lives, they will "shine as lights in the world." The differences in behavior and attitude make the believer stand out against the world's darkness.

The phrase "holding fast" can mean either "holding onto" or "holding out."[2] Believers must do both: hold onto their faith and offer the Word of life to the lost.

DEAR MISSIONARY, you know the truth about Jesus Christ, and your purpose is to offer the beautiful gospel to the lost. Just as our eyes are drawn to the moon because of its brightness against the dark sky, non-believers will be drawn to us and the gospel when we shine with the light of righteousness. Jesus said in Matthew 5:14–16:

> You are the light of the world. A city set on a hill cannot be hidden. Nor do people light a lamp and put it under a basket, but on a stand, and it gives light to all in the house. In the same way, let your light shine before others, so that they may see your

good works and give glory to your Father who is in heaven.

If your attitude and behavior are no different from the world, no one will want to hear what you say, and no one will believe the gospel has the power to change lives. After all, you are no different than they are. Are you compromising and allowing your sin to shame the name of Jesus?

Complaining and arguing also hinder your ability to trust God because they draw your focus away from him and toward your problems. Every time you whine about your situation (which gets exaggerated with each retelling), you demonstrate your lack of faith. Fill your mind with the goodness of God, not the challenges of a temporary world.

How we talk about the challenges in our lives may not seem like a big deal. We call our grumbling "venting" and feel entitled to voice our negative opinions about our host country or the difficulties of the culture we work in, but this is an area where we must guard our testimony. When you experience another delay in the immigration office, shine like a star for the immigration officer with speech "full of grace, seasoned with salt" (Col. 4:6). When circumstances surrounding your ministry seem to put your progress in reverse, maintain a peaceful heart. Your righteous response to this setback may be the very thing God uses as a powerful witness to those around you. Are you keeping a careful watch over your tongue, or has griping and complaining become a habit for you?

DEEP DIVE:

1) Jump ahead to Philippians 4:8. How does this verse about the mind relate to the issue of complaining and arguing?

_____

_____

_____

_____

2) Read 2 Corinthians 2:15–16. What metaphor does Paul use for the Christian in this passage?

_____

_____

_____

_____

3) Read Acts 8:32, which describes Jesus, the Lamb of God, on the way to the cross. How does this description of Jesus relate to the issue of complaining and arguing?

_____

_____

_____

_____

Day 16: Poured Out

"God makes us as broken bread and poured-out wine to
please Him...
Beware of competing calls once the call of God grips you."
~Oswald Chambers[1]

Read Philippians 2:14–18.

In verse 17, Paul referred to himself as a drink offering being
poured out on the sacrifice of the Philippians' faith. To understand this, we must go back to the instructions God gave the
Israelites regarding sacrifices.

In Exodus 29:38–41, God told his people to sacrifice a year-
old lamb, a tenth of an ephah of fine flour mixed with oil, and a

quarter hin of wine on the morning and evening of every day. The wine was the drink offering poured out at the altar.

When the Israelites presented a drink offering to the Lord, they did not set the cup on the altar where it could be picked up and taken back again. The drink offering had to be poured out, so the wine would vaporize and be absorbed by whatever it touched. Gathering the wine back into the cup was impossible because it was wholly consumed while offered to the Lord. Likewise, the animal sacrifice could never be resurrected and added back to a person's flock. Everything offered to the Lord was given irrevocably to him.

God no longer asks us to worship by slaughtering animals and pouring wine on an altar because Christ's sacrifice for our sins is final (Heb. 10), but God does tell us to offer our lives as a sacrifice to him.

Paul wrote in Romans 12:1: "I appeal to you therefore, brothers, by the mercies of God, to present your bodies as a living sacrifice, holy and acceptable to God, which is your spiritual worship."

We face three common temptations in this area. The first is offering part of ourselves to God while holding part in reserve. We are willing to surrender to God's will in *most* areas of our lives but still fight for our own will in others. We don't want to be fully poured out.

The second temptation comes to the person who wants to offer himself to the Lord, but when he begins to feel the heat of suffering, he crawls off the "altar" because God is asking more than the person is willing to give.

Third, someone may present themselves to God but later become distracted by other things that look more satisfying.

All of these are motivated by self-interest. We fear what God may ask of us and want to protect ourselves from pain. We may doubt God is a loving father who does what is best for his children and refuse to entrust ourselves to him. We may forget there is no greater reward than knowing and serving God and that only treasure stored in heaven will last (Matt. 6:19–21).

In verse 17, Paul told the Philippians that being poured out as a sacrifice gave him joy. Paul labored and suffered for the sake of the Philippian church. Instead of seeing the Philippians as being in his debt, he saw his sacrifice as a privilege and opportunity to worship God.

DEAR MISSIONARY, perspective matters. If you look at all your role as a missionary has cost you, your work will become drudgery, and the deadly sin of self-pity will cloud everything you do. But if you view each sacrifice you make as a privilege and a chance to worship your Creator, God will fill you with joy that only comes through willing surrender.

This was Paul's secret. He viewed everything that happened to him as an opportunity to worship. He took his beatings, persecution, chains, and imprisonment and poured them out as an offering to the Lord.

Are you struggling to remain surrendered to God? Are there areas of your life you are withholding from him? Are you afraid of what he might ask of you? When you are tempted to "crawl off the altar," pray for faith like Job, who said amid his trials, "Though he slay me, I will hope in him" (Job 13:15).

Take time to pray about each area of your life where you have sacrificed for the gospel's sake and offer it as a "pleasing aroma" instead of viewing it as an unwelcome intrusion in your life.

DEEP DIVE:

1) Read Luke 9:57–62. What kept each man from immediately and fully following Jesus?

_____

_____

_____

_____

2) Read Matthew 10:37–39. Is something in your life pulling your love away from Jesus?

_____

_____

_____

_____

3) Read Romans 8:12–18. How does this encourage you in your present struggles?

_____

_____

_____

_____

Day 17: Faithful, Focused, and Willing

❧❀❧

"Faithfulness to God is our first obligation in all that we are called
to do in the service of the gospel."
~Iain H. Murray[1]

Read Philippians 2:19–30 and Matthew 25:14–30.

DEAR MISSIONARY, what does God require from you? Did he
give you a number of converts you must make? Or people you
must baptize? Or wells you must dig? We make grand visions for
ministry and dream of all we will achieve, but what God requires
from us is simple: be faithful.

In Jesus' parable in Matthew 25:14–30, the servants were
given different levels of responsibility, yet each had the opportunity to hear, "Well done, good and faithful servant. You have been

faithful over a little; I will set you over much. Enter into the joy of your master."

Two of the servants were faithful and pleased their master. The last was lazy and wasted his opportunity, and instead of praise, he received rebuke and punishment.

In Philippians 2:19–30, Paul commended Timothy and Epaphroditus, setting them before the Philippian church as examples of faithful men.

Timothy had been on Paul's team when he planted the Philippian church (Acts 16). When Paul wrote this letter approximately ten years later, Timothy was still at Paul's side (Phil. 1:1). He did not swerve from the faith and steadily served the various churches where he ministered.

Paul's high praise for Timothy in verses 20 to 22 centers on his genuine concern for the believers. Timothy was not like other Christians who were more concerned with their own interests than the things of Christ. He faithfully prioritized the gospel and the kingdom of God, sacrificing his own interests to serve the Lord.

Epaphroditus, a church member in Philippi, delivered the Philippians' financial gift to Paul in prison. Paul held Epaphroditus in high esteem, calling him a brother, fellow worker, and fellow soldier. Paul's appreciation for Epaphroditus centered on their unity in Christ and common goals for the gospel. Paul told the Philippians to honor men like Epaphroditus because he'd risked his life for the gospel.

Why were these men valuable and productive in the kingdom of God? They were faithful, focused, and willing to sacrifice.

Faithfulness is proven over time but must be built moment by moment. Focus requires keeping one thing at the center while everything else is put to the side. Sacrifice requires selflessness and acceptance of being last and least.

DEAR MISSIONARY, many of us start strong, moving to the mission field prepared to labor morning and night, but as the initial excitement wanes, we begin pursuing personal interests, comforts, and entertainment. Are you as faithful, focused, and willing to sacrifice today as you were when you started your mission work? Are you consistently trying to advance the gospel in your community? Are you tending to your spiritual health and obeying the Lord in the minor issues of your life?

If you have drifted, return to your first love (Rev. 2:4). When you are in awe of Jesus, your love for him will increase, producing fresh strength for enduring faithfulness. Don't get distracted by what others are achieving for Christ. Do what God has called you to, and make it your goal to hear Jesus say, "Well done, good and *faithful* servant." (emphasis mine)

DEEP DIVE:

1) Jump ahead and read Philippians 3:7–14. How does Paul view Christ?

_____

_____

_____

_____

2) How does his view of Christ affect his attitude and behavior?

_____

_____

_____

_____

3) Read Colossians 1:13–20. List and meditate on all of Christ's attributes in these verses. Allow your meditation to draw you closer to him.

_____

_____

_____

_____

4) Read 1 Peter 4:10–11. What is the ultimate reason and motivation for our service to the Lord?

_____

_____

_____

_____

Day 18: Variety for God's Glory

"To reach people we must appreciate and adapt to their culture, but we must also challenge and confront it. This is based on the biblical teaching that all cultures have God's grace and natural revelation in them, yet they are also in rebellious idolatry. If we overadapt to a culture, we have accepted the culture's idols. If, however, we underadapt to a culture, we may have turned our own culture into an idol, an absolute. If we overadapt to a culture, we aren't able to change people because we are not calling them to change. If we underadapt to a culture, no one will be changed because no one will listen to us; we will be confusing, offensive, or simply unpersuasive. To the degree a ministry is overadapted or underadapted to a culture, it loses life-changing power."
~Timothy Keller[1]

Read Philippians 3:1–10.

In verse 2, Paul addressed one of the early church's most significant questions: What must Gentiles do to be saved?

The Book of Acts demonstrated that Jews *and* Gentiles are saved by grace through faith, not through works. But because Christianity grew out of Judaism, some Jewish believers wanted the Gentiles to become Jewish and follow the Laws of Moses, including circumcision, before they could worship together.

Salvation through circumcision may not be an issue you must address in your evangelism, but the danger of putting extra-biblical requirements on someone who wants to follow Jesus is something we need to guard against.

When we preach Jesus, we must remember we are not preaching our own culture or customs. Scripture never tells us to turn a Cambodian into an American or a Tanzanian into an Australian. Scripture corrects sinful aspects of culture, but it never seeks to stop a Kurd from being a Kurd or a Finn from being Finnish.

Instead of viewing our differences as an error to be corrected, we must recognize that our differences come from God, bring him glory, and serve his purposes. God confused the people's languages at the Tower of Babel, dividing them into groups and scattering them over the earth (Gen. 11). Humanity's distinct people groups are his idea.

God places each person on this earth in a particular time and place. He chooses their parents, the culture they were born into, and the language they learn from birth. None of this is a mistake. Instead, it puts God's creativity on display. Eyes, skin, and hair come in a beautiful array of shades. Homes are built from the materials in a specific geographic region, and local dishes are created from God's bounty in different agricultural environments.

In Revelation 7:9 people from every tribe, tongue, and nation gather around God's throne. We maintain our cultural identities even in heaven, so we should not try to change someone from who God made them to be into a poor imitation of ourselves.

DEAR MISSIONARY, pride can infect our attitudes toward others. If you come from a developed country and are serving in an area where people have been doing things the same way for hundreds of years, it's easy to become prideful over the advantages that God—in his grace—gave you.

Having a superior attitude is not winsome and will not draw non-believers to the beauty of Christ. Next time you fall into the trap of comparing your foods, culture, methods, education, socio-economic status, and achievements with those you seek to minister to, remind yourself of the humility Paul taught in Philippians 2. Consider others better than yourself (v. 3) and seek the good of those you minister to instead of spending your time judging them for what you perceive to be their weaknesses.

DEEP DIVE:

1) Read Acts 10. What does Paul realize about who God accepts?

_____

_____

_____

_____

2) What evidence of salvation was demonstrated in the lives of the Gentiles?

_____

_____

_____

_____

3) Read Acts 11:1–18. What was the Jewish believers' initial response to Peter's actions in Acts 10? What was their response by the time Peter finished his explanation?

_____

_____

_____

_____

4) Reflect on Peter's vision in Acts 10:9–16. What did it teach Peter and the other Jewish believers about their dietary laws?

_____

_____

_____

_____

5) What does it teach us today regarding culture and the gospel?

_____

_____

_____

_____

Day 19: Put No Confidence in the Flesh

"God will not go forth with that man who marches in his own strength."

~Charles Spurgeon[1]

Read Philippians 3:1–11.

In verse 2, Paul warned the Philippians to watch out for "those dogs" who mutilate the flesh. Paul was referring to the Jews who taught that Gentiles had to be circumcised to be saved. This teaching denied that salvation is by grace through faith in Jesus and not by works of the flesh.

Using himself as an example, Paul listed all the qualifications that gave him prestige among the Jews. Yet when he met Christ, Paul realized all his reasons for boasting about himself were "rubbish." They couldn't save him and gained him nothing in God's kingdom.

Three times in two verses, Paul used the words "loss" or "lost," yet instead of mourning, he rejoiced that he could rebuild his identity around Christ's victory on the cross instead of his works of the flesh. He was now "in Christ" and possessed Christ's righteousness through faith.

Christianity is the only faith in the world that isn't built on a works-based righteousness. Instead of relying on a person's accomplishments, which leads to pride, the Kingdom of God requires humble trust in Christ and his death on the cross. The gospel is simple, yet it causes many people to stumble because, in their pride, they either deny they need a savior or want to save themselves.

DEAR MISSIONARY, even if you accurately preach that salvation is by faith and not by works, it's easy to slip into trusting your abilities as you minister. You may feel you are a good missionary because of your intellectual capacity to learn languages. You may rely more heavily on your knowledge of Greek and Hebrew than the power of the Holy Spirit when translating Scripture. You may depend on your charisma and public-speaking skills to hold an audience captive as you preach on the street corner. You may think your endurance on the field is due to your own stamina or that the success of your church plant is due to your own wisdom. Pride may lead you to applaud yourself for succeeding where others have failed.

Sometimes, we need a reality check: We can do nothing apart from God. We cannot draw a breath or blink an eye unless God allows us. Intellect, wit, charm, and memory can be taken instantly. Every work will be tested by the fire of God's judgment

(1 Cor. 3:10–15), and anything done in human strength and wisdom will burn.

We must acknowledge our inability to do anything and depend on the Holy Spirit, who calls, equips, enables, empowers, and produces fruit. Only his accomplishments have eternal value —trust in him, not your flesh.

DEEP DIVE:

1) Read 1 Corinthians 3:10–15, Revelation 22:12, and Matthew 25:14–30. What do you learn about the "bema" seat judgment?

_____

_____

_____

_____

2) Read 2 Peter 1:3–9. What will make you effective and productive in your knowledge of the Lord Jesus Christ? Where do each of these qualities come from? See Galatians 5:22–23.

_____

_____

_____

_____

3) How do Jeremiah 17:10 and Revelation 2:23 describe God?

_____

_____

_____

_____

Day 20: To Know Christ

"Outside of Christ, I am only a sinner, but in Christ, I am saved.
Outside of Christ, I am empty; in Christ, I am full. Outside of
Christ, I am weak; in Christ, I am strong. Outside of Christ, I
cannot; in Christ, I am more than able. Outside of Christ, I have
been defeated; in Christ, I am already victorious. How meaningful
are the words, 'in Christ.'"
~Watchman Nee[1]

Read Philippians 3:7–11.

Paul taught in the first half of Chapter Three that we cannot earn
our salvation through works. Salvation is only through faith in
Christ and his death on the cross. Believers "put on" Christ's
righteousness and are justified through him.

Once they know they are going to heaven, many believers stop there, satisfied with a shallow Christian life. Like a child who opens an expensive gift, sets it aside, and begins playing with the box, these Christians focus on the benefits they receive from Christ instead of Christ himself.

But for Paul, salvation was not the primary goal of Christianity—Christ was. Paul was not content with theological head-knowledge about Jesus, though this is important. Paul yearned for intimate fellowship with Jesus and wanted the beauty of Christ to fill his entire vision. His desire for Jesus pushed everything else out of the way. This was why he could "count all things loss." He rightly recognized that nothing compared with knowing the Savior.

How can *you* know Christ? Paul answered this question in these verses.

First, evaluate what you love. Jesus said, "For where your treasure is, there your heart will be also" (Matt. 6:21). Are you still treasuring "rubbish" above Christ? Anything you love more than Jesus counts as rubbish. You must be willing to give up anything that takes Christ's rightful place in your heart.

Second, you need to know Christ and the power of his resurrection. God's power raised Christ from the dead, and this same power is available to every believer through the Holy Spirit (Eph. 1:19–20). His power is the only way to do anything worthwhile (see Day 20), and your intimacy with Christ will grow when you live through his power and not your own.

Third, you must realize that some aspects of fellowship with Christ are only attainable through suffering. This is why Paul rejoiced when he suffered—it gave him a closeness to Christ that could not be gained any other way. To suffer for him is to know him.

Fourth, you must be willing to be conformed to Christ's death. Though this includes death to selfish desires, Paul spoke of Christ's physical death and was ready to die for Christ's sake. If death as a martyr could help him know and honor Jesus, he rejoiced in the opportunity. To Paul, death was gain (Phil. 1:21).

Paul took us through the progression of Christ's experience on earth: He suffered, he died, and then he was resurrected. Paul, who wished to follow his Savior, was willing to suffer and die, knowing that he, too, would be resurrected from the dead (1 Thess. 4:13–17).

DEAR MISSIONARY, Jesus is everything, but we often lack Paul's burning passion for Jesus because we are either content with a shallow relationship with him or too busy with the idols in our lives.

Your effectiveness as a missionary is connected to your personal longing to know Christ. Henry Martyn, a missionary to India, said, "The spirit of Christ is the spirit of missions. The nearer we get to him, the more intensely missionary we become."[2]

You cannot convince unbelievers that Christ is glorious and deserves all worship if you do not treasure him above all else. If you have not picked up your cross to follow Him, neither will they.

Christ must fill your vision. You must passionately esteem Christ before leading others to do the same. A small view of Christ leads to weak preaching, frequent compromise, and a dull Christian life. But a missionary who holds Christ as his "all in all" will galvanize others to do the same.

DEEP DIVE:

1) What does 2 Peter 1:3 tell you about the "knowledge" of Christ?

_____

_____

_____

_____

2) How and why is this knowledge beneficial?

_____

_____

_____

_____

3) Read Ephesians 1:15–23. What does the "Spirit of wisdom and of revelation" (v. 17) do to the believer's heart? What will the believer then know?

_____

_____

_____

_____

4) What did the power of God do for Christ?

_____

_____

_____

_____

5) How do believers participate in this power?

_____

_____

_____

_____

6) Consider this quotation from C. A. Coates regarding Paul's longing for Christ. How does it challenge your relationship with Christ?

> The knowledge of Christ in glory was the supreme desire of Paul's heart, and this desire could never exist without producing an intense longing to reach Him in the place where He is. Hence, the heart that longs after Him instinctively turns to the path by which he reached that place in glory, and earnestly desires to reach Him in that place by the very path which He trod. The heart asks, "How did He reach that glory? Was it through resurrection? And did not sufferings and death necessarily precede resurrection?" Then the heart says, "Nothing would please me so well as to reach Him in resurrection glory by the very path which took Him there." It is the martyr spirit. Paul wanted to tread as a martyr the pathway of suffering and death, that he might reach resurrection and glory by the same path as the blessed One who had won his heart.[3]

Day 21: Press On

"Complacency is a deadly foe of all spiritual growth."
~A. W. Tozer[1]

Read Philippians 3:12–16.

Paul wrote in Philippians 3:7–11 that he wanted to "know Christ." This was the aim Paul referred to in verse 14 when he said, "I press on toward the goal."

Knowing Christ and growing in a relationship with him is an ongoing process. God is infinite, and we know little of all that he is. His ways and thoughts are above ours (Isa. 55:8–9), and his understanding is unsearchable (Isa. 40:28). Yet God has revealed himself through his Son. Jesus said, "And whoever sees me sees him who sent me" (John 12:45). The more we know Jesus, the more we know the Father.

One aspect of knowing Christ is being conformed to his image (Rom. 8:29; 1 John 3:2). This is the reason Christ "laid hold" of Paul and the same reason he lays hold of us. God's will is that we become like his Son, so Paul aligned his will with God's and strove to "lay hold" of the holiness God wanted for him.

Sanctification is a process that continues throughout our lives. Paul explained this in Philippians 1:6: "And I am sure of this, that he who began a good work in you will bring it to completion at the day of Jesus Christ." Paul knew God wasn't done sanctifying him, which he noted when he said: "Not that I have already obtained this or am already perfect" (v. 12) and "I do not consider that I have made it my own" (v. 13).

Paul's perspective is helpful for us. When he looked at how far he still needed to go in his Christian life, he didn't get discouraged and quit pursuing Christ. Instead, he decided to "press on." Following Jesus is, indeed, a long obedience in the same direction.[2] The Christian life is not achieved in a momentary flash of glory but in the slow and steady progress of walking with Christ and drawing closer to him daily.

The Christian life is not easy, and sometimes we fail, but Paul told us to handle our failures by "forgetting what lies behind." Wallowing in shame and guilt over past sins that Christ's blood has already cleansed you from will discourage you. Walk in the freedom from condemnation Christ gave the believer.

Even spiritual successes must be left behind. If the Holy Spirit worked through you to achieve something for the kingdom, praise God, and make yourself available to him for the next thing he puts in front of you (Eph. 2:10). Staring too long at past successes can lead to pride and apathy. We should not be content with what we have done because there is still too much left to do.

Dear missionary, do not be content with your progress in the faith, but strive to walk more closely with Christ today than yesterday. There is always more of Christ to know; deeper fellowship with him is the "prize" given to those who persevere.

Pressing on toward Jesus and striving for spiritual growth requires self-discipline because the things of the Spirit are contrary to those of the flesh. Pressing on toward Christ is not an abstract concept; examining your habits will tell you if you are genuinely pursuing Christ. How much time and effort do you give daily to prayer and meditating on the Scriptures? Are you memorizing the Word and hiding it in your heart? Are you quick to confess sin and change, or do you ignore the conviction of the Holy Spirit?

Do not be discouraged if you find your spiritual disciplines are lacking. Forget what is behind and "reach forward to those things which are ahead." You cannot change yesterday, but you can pursue Christ today.

Galatians 6:7–9 says:

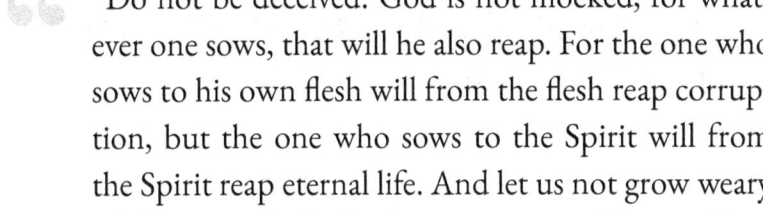

> "Do not be deceived: God is not mocked, for whatever one sows, that will he also reap. For the one who sows to his own flesh will from the flesh reap corruption, but the one who sows to the Spirit will from the Spirit reap eternal life. And let us not grow weary of doing good, for in due season we will reap, if we do not give up."

You, dear missionary, will reap if you press on and do not give up.

DEEP DIVE:

1) Read 1 Corinthians 9:24–27 and Hebrews 12:1–17. List the instructions each verse gives you for "running" the Christian race.

_____

_____

_____

_____

2) Read 1 Timothy 6:11–16. Paul told Timothy to "fight" for the faith. From these verses, how was Timothy supposed to "fight?"

_____

_____

_____

_____

3) If you don't already have one, make a plan for your personal spiritual disciplines. Which book of the Bible will you begin studying in depth? Which Scriptures will you memorize in the coming month? How much time will you commit to prayer? How much time will you spend in fellowship with other believers, receiving and giving accountability?

_____

_____

_____

_____

Day 22: Don't Lose Ground

"Brethren, it is easier to declaim against a thousand sins of others,
than to mortify one sin in ourselves."
~John Flavel[1]

Read Philippians 3:12–16.

Christianity is a process of continual change as the Holy Spirit
refines us, rooting out hidden sin and conforming us to the image
of Christ. In verse 16, Paul pointed out a challenge to sanctification: not living up to the standard we have attained. We know the
truth but fail to obey. Instead of moving forward, we slip
backward.

In Philippians 2:12, Paul commands the Philippians to "work
out your own salvation with fear and trembling" (see Day 14). You

must do the same. Are you producing fruit in accordance with your salvation? Are you moving toward Christ or away from him?

DEAR MISSIONARY, today we will use Paul's epistle to the Philippians for self-reflection. The same admonishments and encouragements Paul gave them apply to us.

Read the Scripture reference for each point, and allow God's Word to speak to you. Do not rush through the list, but make each point an opportunity for prayer, and allow the Holy Spirit to show you where you might be weak or straying from the faith. Be quick to repent if you find yourself in error, and resist the temptation to make excuses or justify your sin.

If you resist the devil in these areas, he will flee from you (Jas. 4:7), but if you hide sin in your heart, you give the devil a foothold (Eph. 4:27).

Pray, then read and reflect:

1. Are you in competition with other believers or missionaries? (Phil. 1:15–18)
2. Are you performing for the praise of men instead of having integrity in all aspects of life? (Phil. 1:27)
3. Are you causing or allowing division in the church instead of standing as one in Christ with fellow believers or missionaries? (Phil. 1:27; Phil 2:1–2)
4. Are you giving way to fear instead of living boldly for Christ? (Phil. 1:28)
5. Are you running from suffering instead of embracing it as a means of fellowship with Christ? (Phil. 1:29; Phil. 3:10)
6. Are you allowing pride and selfishness to dictate how you treat others? (Phil. 2:3–4)

7. Are you living with the "mind of Christ" in humility and obedience? (Phil. 2:5–11)

8. Do you regularly give time to self-examination? (Phil. 2:12)

9. Do you complain and argue or maintain a submitted heart? (Phil. 2:14)

10. Are you willing to be "poured out" for the cause of Christ, or do you resist being a living sacrifice? (Phil. 2:17)

11. Do you put self-interest above the things of Christ? (Phil. 2:21)

12. Do you regard your life above Christ? (Phil. 2:30)

13. Do you trust in the flesh? (Phil. 3:3)

14. Have you torn down every idol in your life and made knowing Christ your greatest passion? (Phil. 3:7–11)

15. Are you pressing on in the faith? (Phil. 3:12–16)

16. Are you living as an enemy of the cross of Christ? (Phil. 3:17–19)

17. Are you living like a citizen of heaven? (Phil. 3:20)

18. Are you rejoicing in the Lord in every circumstance? (Phil. 4:4)

19. Are you treating others with gentleness? (Phil. 4:5)

20. Are you worrying or praying? (Phil. 4:6–7)

21. Are you guarding your thoughts and renewing your mind? (Phil. 4:8)

22. Are you content in all circumstances? (Phil. 4:11–13)

23. Are you generous with your resources, especially with other believers? (Phil. 4:14)

Pressing on instead of falling backward requires discipline. The battle is not won in a moment.

Stay the course.

DEEP DIVE:

1) Read Galatians 6:3–4. What does Paul warn against, and what are we told to do?

_____

_____

_____

_____

2) How can you apply this to your life today?

_____

_____

_____

_____

3) Read Psalm 66:18. What happens when we cherish iniquity in our hearts?

_____

_____

_____

_____

4) What does Jesus say about obedience in John 14:15?

_____

_____

_____

_____

Day 23: Enemies of Christ

"All heaven is interested in the cross of Christ, all hell terribly afraid of it, while men are the only beings who more or less ignore its meaning."
~Oswald Chambers[1]

Read Philippians 3:17–21.

There are only two categories of people in the world: those who are "in Christ" and those who are his enemies. This may sound harsh, but Jesus told the Pharisees they were of their "father the devil" (John 8:44), and Paul called the false prophet Elymas a "son of the devil and enemy of all righteousness" (Acts 13:10).

Colossians 1:13–21 explains that the unbeliever is "alienated and hostile" and belongs to the "domain of darkness," while believers have been transferred to "the kingdom of his beloved Son."

James 4:4 declares that "friendship with the world is enmity with God." There is no middle ground. People are either with God or against him.

In Philippians 3:19, Paul describes the "enemies of the cross of Christ" in four ways. First, "their end is destruction." Salvation is only through Jesus' sacrificial death on the cross, so anyone who opposes or minimizes the cross has rejected God's provision for redemption and will face eternal damnation.

Second, Paul wrote that "their god is their belly." This does not refer only to food, as "belly" means "appetite" and can refer to any desire for physical pleasure.[2] These people lived to indulge and satisfy their lusts.

Third, Paul said they "glory in their shame," pridefully flaunting and rejoicing in the sin that should have caused humiliation. How easy this is to recognize today, where sin is celebrated as good!

Finally, Paul wrote that they have their "minds set on earthly things." These people were concerned with being successful and satisfied in this present world without considering the life to come.

In direct contrast, Paul reminded the Philippians that they are citizens of heaven and must not live as enemies of the very cross that "opened" heaven to them. Being a citizen of heaven requires that they deny their sinful lusts and celebrate Christ, not sin.

Believers were to focus on heaven and "eagerly wait" (NKJV) for their Savior. To wait "eagerly" literally means to "thrust forward the head and neck as in anxious expectation of hearing or seeing something."[3] Believers must long for the Savior and the day we will be with him in glorious bodies like his. All we have with Jesus in heaven is far better than what this world can offer.

DEAR MISSIONARY, the cross is offensive to those who love darkness. People do not like admitting they are sinners in need of a Savior, and Christ's demand of absolute surrender is a stumbling block for those who want to do what is right in their own eyes. The cross is foolishness to those who are perishing (1 Cor. 1:18), but preach it anyway.

Do not become an enemy of the cross of Christ yourself by preaching anything other than the true gospel. It is not your job to make the gospel palatable or to "ease" people into faith. Do not teach empty religion and build a "church" full of false converts.

Jesus will not share his throne with anyone. He is the way, the truth, and the life (John 14:6). There is no salvation apart from him.

We must not be naive and think that there are no enemies of the cross within the church. Church leaders and even missionaries may live as enemies, pursuing fleshly lusts, justifying and approving sin, and loving the things of the world. We must be set apart. We belong to heaven.

Let today's Scriptures be a point of reflection, both for *what* you preach and *how* you live. Are you living as an enemy of the cross of Christ?

DEEP DIVE:

1) Any doctrine that does not elevate Christ, the cross, Jesus' death, and his resurrection opposes the gospel. Satan attacks Christ's deity, power, and authority to make the cross seem pointless. False doctrines teach that *the cross never happened*, that *it is not necessary*, or that *it is not enough*. Examine the beliefs of the religion that is prevalent where you minister. How does it seek to destroy or ignore the cross? ("Christian" churches are not immune to false doctrines. If you are in a "Christian setting," evaluate the teachings of the churches around you. Are they teaching anything in error?)

_____

_____

_____

_____

2) Read 1 John 2:1–6 and meditate on verse 6. Are there changes you need to make in your life so that you behave as Jesus did?

_____

_____

_____

_____

3) For further study regarding Christ's second coming and the transformation of our earthly bodies into heavenly bodies, read 1 Corinthians 15:51–56, 1 Thessalonians 4:13–18, and 1 John 3:2–3. What does John say that everyone who hopes will do?

_____

_____

_____

_____

Day 24: Agree with Each Other in the Lord

"Satan always hates Christian fellowship; it is his policy to keep Christians apart. Anything which can divide saints from one another he delights in. He attaches far more importance to godly intercourse than we do. Since union is strength, he does his best to promote separation."
~Charles Spurgeon[1]

Read Philippians 4:1–3 and Matthew 18:15–20.

How embarrassing for Euodia and Syntyche to have their names recorded in Scripture for quarreling and to have us, all these years later, reading about their drama!

The Bible doesn't explain why they were fighting, but their

disagreement was bad enough for Paul to address it from hundreds of miles away. His letter was read aloud to the entire church, and these women were called out in front of everyone.

This may offend your modern idea of privacy, but it follows the principles for conflict resolution Jesus laid out in Matthew 18:15–20. When believers have a dispute, they must go to each other to seek forgiveness and reconciliation. If they cannot settle their differences one-on-one, they must invite witnesses into the conversation to help them make peace. If this fails, the issue must be brought to the church, which collectively seeks to persuade them to repent and reconcile. If they still refuse to agree, they are put outside the fellowship until they repent, at which time their fellowship is restored.

Here, we see this process in action. Paul pleaded with Euodia and Syntyche to settle their differences and agree with each other. He requested his "true companion"[2] ("loyal yokefellow" in NIV)[3] to help them reconcile. It appears the conflict reached the point where the women would not agree without help. Blinded by self-righteousness, their division was damaging the church.

The key to Paul's plea to these women was the phrase "in the Lord." These powerful words reminded the women of their true identities. As believers, they were "in Christ," sharing in the fellowship of the Holy Spirit, and would spend eternity together in heaven, worshiping God in perfect unity.

The only thing hindering unity on earth is sin. Sin breaks Christian fellowship, damages churches, and wounds hearts. This is why Paul urged these women to reconcile and told the Philippians to have the mind of Christ (Phil. 2:5), who acted out of humility and genuine love.

DEAR MISSIONARY, the gospel proclaims reconciliation between God and man. In this way, our mission as ambassadors of Christ is one of peacemaking. Jesus said, "Blessed are the peacemakers, for they will be called children of God" (Matt. 5:9), yet many missionaries do not take their ministry as peacemakers seriously. They let pride rule their lives and bitterness fill their hearts.

In Galatians 12:15, Paul warned that when a root of bitterness springs up, it defiles many. The missionary who harbors bitterness or resentment in his heart and refuses to reconcile damages the church he came to build and serve.

Our peace with God must be demonstrated in our lives. We show we are "in Christ" when we unite with other believers, show patience, and give and receive forgiveness. We cannot effectively preach Christ if we do not walk in the Holy Spirit's power and love one another.

Making peace requires effort, time, patience, wisdom, endurance, active listening, honest communication, humility, and forgiveness. You may be tempted to ignore this aspect of your Christian life, but you must not. If you speak of Christ's peace, you must live it.*

Are you hiding bitterness in your heart toward another believer? Are there wounds in your missionary community or church that need to be addressed and covered with the love and forgiveness of Christ? Do not wait for someone else to take the lead in reconciliation. Walk in obedience and be a peacemaker.

DEEP DIVE:

1) Read 2 Corinthians 5:16–21. What does it teach you about being "in Christ" and the Christian's work as an ambassador?

_____

_____

_____

_____

2) Read 1 Corinthians 6:1–7 and Matthew 5:23–26. According to these verses, how are believers to handle disputes?

_____

_____

_____

_____

3) What attitude should a believer have when wronged? Why?

_____

_____

_____

_____

4) Are there any situations in your life where you have been waiting for someone else to take the lead in reconciliation? According to Scripture, what should you do in the situation?

_____

_____

_____

_____

*I am not advocating that anyone remain in a situation where they are repeatedly harmed or reconcile with a dangerous person. Repentance and actual change are a necessary part of reconciliation. If someone's behavior does not change, their repentance is not genuine and must be dealt with according to Matthew 18:15–20. It may reach the point where the unrepentant person is put outside of the fellowship, or the relationship is completely broken off.

Day 25: Rejoice

❦

"Joy is distinctly a Christian word and a Christian thing. It is the reverse of happiness. Happiness is the result of what happens of an agreeable sort. Joy has its springs deep down inside. And that spring never runs dry, no matter what happens. Only Jesus gives that joy. He had joy, singing its music within, even under the shadow of the cross. It is an unknown word and thing except as He has sway within."
~S.D. Gordon[1]

Read Philippians 4:1–9.

Philippians is called the epistle of joy because "joy" or "rejoice" appear more than fifteen times.

We desire joy because it rejuvenates and energizes our hearts.

Nehemiah 8:10 says, "The joy of the Lord is your strength." On the contrary, Psalms and Proverbs speak of how sorrow dims the eyes, crushes the heart, melts the spirit, and decays the bones (Ps. 31:10).

For many of us, joy feels elusive because we look for it in our circumstances, which are constantly changing. If situations turn out favorably, we celebrate, but when life's challenges come, we react with anger and frustration and wallow in discontent. Finding joy in temporal circumstances does not work because what we gain can be lost just as quickly.

True joy comes from God, which is why Paul commanded three times in the book of Philippians: "Rejoice in the Lord" (3:1, 4:4, 4:10). He also said to "rejoice in Jesus Christ" (1:26) and "rejoice in the faith" (1:25).

Our rejoicing must be centered on Jesus, and our joy should never vacillate because joy is a fruit of the Holy Spirit (Gal. 5:22), and he is a constant presence in our lives.

How do you rejoice in the Lord?

First, rejoice in God's nature. He is reliable, faithful, trustworthy, and compassionate. He is slow to anger and abounds in love. He is omnipotent, omnipresent, and omniscient. He never fails. Rejoice that God is good.

Second, rejoice in what God has done for you. Jesus died for your sins and reconciled you to the Father. He gave you eternal life and prepared a place for you in heaven. He has given you a new nature and clothed you with his righteousness. He has given you a helper and comforter, the Holy Spirit, who provides wisdom and leads you into truth.

Paul directed us to rejoice in these things because they are eternal, not temporal. God will never fail, so we always have reasons to rejoice.

When we "lose" our joy, it isn't because God changed; the problem is our focus. We look at our circumstances and worry instead of looking at our Savior. Colossians 3:2 says, "Set your minds on things that are above, not on things that are on earth." In Philippians 4:8–9, Paul instructed us to think about what is true, noble, right, pure, lovely, admirable, excellent, and praiseworthy. Aren't these words a perfect description of our Lord Jesus Christ?

DEAR MISSIONARY, you must pay attention to your own joy. Ministry work is draining and discouraging, and you will sometimes be tempted to give up. How will you endure? Where does your strength come from?

"The joy of the Lord is your strength" (Neh. 8:10). If you lose your joy, you lose your strength. Consider this quotation from A. B. Simpson: "Begin to rejoice in the Lord, and your bones will flourish like an herb, and your cheeks will glow with the bloom of health and freshness. Worry, fear, distrust, care—all are poisonous! Joy is balm and healing, and if you will but rejoice, God will give power."[2]

You must "re-fill" your strength daily by rejoicing in Jesus and spending time in His Word and prayer. If you do not purposely focus your mind and affection on Jesus, you will work in your own strength and be overwhelmed by your circumstances. Self-care is essential, and no aspect of it is as important as your spiritual life. You will face times of sorrow, but even when the world seems at its darkest, Christ is worth celebrating.

"Rejoice in the Lord always; again I will say, rejoice!"

DEEP DIVE:

1) Make a "reasons to rejoice in the Lord" list. Post the list, refer to it often, and add to it as you come across new reasons to rejoice in the Lord.

_____

_____

_____

_____

2) Read Habakkuk 3:17–19. How does Habakkuk's prayer instruct you to respond to the challenges in your life?

_____

_____

_____

_____

3) Jump ahead to Philippians 4:10–13. How does contentment relate to joy?

_____

_____

_____

_____

Day 26: The Path to Peace

"Blessed are the single-hearted, for they shall enjoy much peace...
If you refuse to be hurried and pressed, if you stay your soul on
God, nothing can keep you from that clearness of spirit which is
life and peace. In that stillness you know what His will is."
~Amy Carmichael, missionary to India[1]

Read Philippians 4:4–9.

Anxiety is crippling because it chokes our joy, saps our strength,
and erodes our confidence, leaving us hopeless and helpless.
Anxiety may seem like an unavoidable part of life, but we are not
obligated to live in distress.

Isaiah 26:3–4 says:

You keep him in perfect peace
whose mind is stayed on you,
because he trusts in you.
Trust in the Lord forever,
for the Lord God is an everlasting rock.

God promises perfect peace to all who trust in the Lord and focus on him. Anxiety results from being distracted by our problems and taking our eyes off Christ. As our focus on God fluctuates, so does our peace.

Focusing on Christ begins with rejoicing *in the Lord* and not seeking joy in circumstances. God's faithfulness and goodness never change; we always have reasons to rejoice in him.

At first glance, reasonableness (*gentleness* in NKJV, NIV) may not seem related to peace, but anxiety or fear may lead someone who isn't trusting God to aggressively and *unreasonably* fight for his own interests. However, someone with a peaceful, trusting heart will respond gently (verse 5), knowing God is his defender and helper in times of trouble. Gentleness should characterize a Christian's interaction with everyone (Rom. 12:18).

Verse 5 ended with a reminder that Jesus will soon return, which puts everything in perspective. When he comes, the worries of this life will end. Jesus will judge with absolute justice, and everything will happen according to his sovereign plan (Mark 13:32; Rom. 12:19).

Anxiety stems from doubt in God's ability to care for his children, but we must not be anxious about anything (verse 6) since God is both sovereign and good and holds us in his hands.

Instead of worrying, we must connect with Christ—the

Prince of Peace—through prayer and bring our specific petitions to him. We are welcome to come boldly before God's throne as his children (Heb. 4:16). If we ask for bread, will he give us a stone (Matt. 7:9–11)? He answers beyond what we can ask or think (Eph. 3:20).

What is the outcome for a rejoicing, gentle Christian who looks to Christ with expectation and prays about everything with thankfulness?

The Holy Spirit produces a supernatural peace in his life (Gal. 5:22), which is beyond human understanding. Even amid the worst trials, God's peace will guard a Christian's mind and heart from despair, doubt, and Satan's lies.

DEAR MISSIONARY, life is challenging, and enjoying God's perfect peace may seem impossible with the added stresses of ministry. We live like people drowning in the ocean; before one wave of problems is resolved, another is upon us.

Our lives and ministries will be much healthier if we respond to difficulties with spontaneous prayers that spring from a mind saturated with God's Word instead of panicking in distress. What issue are you facing now that you have failed to pray about?

When Paul was in prison in Philippi, his automatic response was to pray and worship (Acts 16). He did not have to think about what to do because he had a daily habit of turning to Jesus with everything. How will you create a habit of turning to God with everything?

Charles Spurgeon said, "A Bible that is falling apart usually belongs to someone who isn't."[2] We must not wait until a crisis hits to build our faith if we want the supernatural peace of God.

Take time today to rejoice that Christ is soon returning, and allow this truth to adjust your perspective. How much smaller and insignificant do your problems look after you have focused on and celebrated Christ?

Christ's second coming is an essential aspect of the gospel. He will judge sinners and resurrect his people. Do you remember to include this in your preaching?

DEEP DIVE:

1) Read Ephesians 6:10–18. What items of the armor mentioned in Ephesians do you see in Philippians 4:4–9?

_____

_____

_____

_____

2) How do they all work together in a believer's life?
Read John 14:25–27. What does the Prince of Peace say about peace?

_____

_____

_____

_____

3) Why is Jesus called the Prince of Peace?

_____

_____

_____

_____

4) How does 2 Timothy 1:7 encourage you?

_____

_____

_____

_____

Day 27: Think

"The difference between worldliness and godliness is a renewed mind."
~Edwin W. Lutzer[1]

Read Philippians 4:4–9.

In verse 8, Paul addressed a critical aspect of the Christian life: the mind. God gave humans the ability to reason, create, daydream, imagine, store memories, process language, and love Him (Mark 12:30). Our intelligence is a great strength, but it is also a great weakness, depending on whether we control our thoughts or they control us.

Our minds were corrupted during the fall (Gen. 3), which made our thinking futile (Eph. 4:17; Rom. 1:21) and hostile to

Christ (Rom. 8:7). Unless we renew our minds in God's truth (Rom. 12:1–2), we will fixate on the desires of the flesh and be deceived by Satan's lies.

We renew our minds when we *decide* to "take every thought captive and make it obedient to Christ" (2 Cor. 10:5) instead of allowing our minds to carry us wherever they want.

What does an obedient thought look like? It meditates on things Christ approves of—things that are true, honorable, just, pure, lovely, commendable, excellent, and praiseworthy.

Scripture is the infallible, final authority on God's truth. When Scripture shines on our thoughts, it identifies whether we believe the truth or are deceived. Satan is the father of lies (John 8:44) and uses deception as a weapon against us. If we do not test our thoughts against Scripture, we will fall victim to his schemes to kill, steal, and destroy (John 10:10). But a mind that is aligned with Scripture gives a believer discernment, so he will know God's good, pleasing, and acceptable will (Rom. 12:2).

Renewing your mind is a continual practice requiring vigilance. When a wrong thought enters your mind, you must be aware of the danger and divert your thinking back to the things of God. Memorizing Scripture is a powerful way to keep your mind focused on Christ.

Don't miss the connection between verses 7 and 8. A mind guarded by the peace of God will think Christ-honoring thoughts, which in turn will produce greater peace. Such a person is continually strengthened and built up in truth.

DEAR MISSIONARY, you must hold Scripture in high esteem and proclaim the *whole* counsel of the Word of God (Acts. 20:27). People's minds can only be renewed to the extent that they have learned his truth. Weak preaching and watered-down theology do not serve anyone. But a mind that has the opportunity to feast on God's Word will be radically reoriented to the things of God. Culture is changed one renewed mind at a time.

Thought patterns run deep, and changing them requires awareness and effort. As an outsider to the culture you work in, it may be easier for you to recognize where Satan has deceived people for generations. You must help believers combat Satan's lies with the truth. If you minister within your own culture, you must be an example of someone who thinks and behaves differently, demonstrating the fruit of a renewed mind in your life.

Do your thoughts please God? Is the entertainment you choose lovely, pure, excellent, and praiseworthy? You reap what you sow (Gal. 6:7–9). If you sow to the flesh, you will live a defeated Christian life. But if you plant God's Word in your heart, you will be victorious.

Your faithfulness in taking your thoughts captive will affect your ability to help others do the same. How will you take the speck out of your brother's eye if you have not removed the plank from your own (Matt. 7:1–5)? If you are not walking in obedience to Christ, you will struggle to help others do so, hindering your effectiveness in making disciples.

If this is an area of difficulty for you, remember that God is working in you to complete what he started and will help you be victorious.

DEEP DIVE:

1) Read Romans 8:5–8. Make two columns labeled "Flesh" and "Spirit." List all the descriptions of a person ruled by the flesh and a person led by the Spirit.

_____

_____

_____

_____

2) Read Ephesians 4:17–23. Add these descriptions to the columns you created for Question One.

_____

_____

_____

_____

3) Read Proverbs 3:5–8, Proverbs 12:8, and Proverbs 28:26. How will you pursue God's wisdom today?

_____

_____

_____

_____

Day 28: Contentment

"The secret is Christ in me, not me in a different set of
circumstances."
~Elisabeth Elliot, widowed missionary to Ecuador[1]

Read Philippians 4:10–13.

Today's passage contains one of the Bible's most quoted and
misapplied Scriptures, Philippians 4:13, which says, "I can do all
things through Christ who strengthens me." (NKJV)

Marathon runners and mountain climbers recite this verse as
they strive to achieve their athletic goals, while others print it on
their clothing or paint it on their walls for inspiration.

It's okay to find encouragement in this Scripture because
Christ is, ultimately, the source of all our strength. He gives us

"life and breath and everything" and "in him we live and move and have our being" (Acts 17:22–28). However, if we fail to read this Scripture in context, we miss that Paul was referring to one of the most challenging things for believers: being content in any circumstance.

In verse 10, Paul expressed his thankfulness for the financial gift the Philippians sent him. He was not asking for another donation or accusing them of being slow to help. Instead, he assured them he was okay because he had learned to be content in any situation, whether he was experiencing the hunger of poverty or had plenty and his stomach was full.

He then gave the secret for his contentment: "I can do all things through Christ who strengthens me."

It's easy to be content when life is comfortable. When things are difficult, we reject our situation by fighting or running from it, not realizing we are rebelling against God's sovereignty. We think we deserve better and ask God, "Why me?" Such grumbling comes from a heart full of self-pity and pride and erodes our joy and strength.

Christians experience contentment when they accept that God sovereignly allowed their situation and choose to trust him, even when they do not understand how he will work all things for good.

God uses everything in our lives to sanctify us, and we only mature when we endure trials (Jas. 1). As we walk faithfully with Jesus through every hardship, we get to watch God unfold his will in us and for us. Paul was content, even in prison, because his chains were for the benefit of the gospel, and everything he experienced glorified Christ.

We can learn to be content only through enduring trials with a thankful, trusting heart.

First, you must rejoice in the Lord. Focus on God's goodness instead of your problems.

Second, pray about everything. God's peace will guard your heart and mind from resentment and a sour attitude.

Third, capture thoughts that are not obedient to Christ and refuse to dwell on your difficulties. As you think about God's character, your trust in him will increase, and you will be strengthened in your resolve to follow Jesus even in the dark times.

DEAR MISSIONARY, no doubt, as you read this, you are in a situation where you feel discontented. You may be struggling with a difficult marriage or an exhausting parent-child relationship. What is God accomplishing *in you* as you live through your struggles?

Your challenge might be daily life without modern conveniences, which wears you down. Can you find joy as you light a candle because the power has gone out again?

You may be exhausted from cultural stress that strains your nerves. Can you rejoice in another cup of tea prepared for yet another visitor who arrived at a very wrong time and wants more from you than you can give?

Whatever your situation is, do not be anxious about it, but pray. God gives strength to the weak. He will never leave you or forsake you. He will lift your countenance and shine his light on you.

Ask him.

DEEP DIVE:

1) Read 2 Corinthians 4:16–18. Paul called the trials of this life
"light momentary affliction." What advice does Paul give in these
verses for enduring suffering? How can you apply this in your life
today?

_____

_____

_____

_____

2) Read the blessing God instructed Moses and Aaron to speak to
the Israelites in Numbers 6:22–26. How does it encourage you?

_____

_____

_____

_____

3) How do your weaknesses benefit you spiritually? Read
1 Corinthians 1:26–31 and 1 Corinthians 12:7–10.

_____

_____

_____

_____

Day 29: He Will Supply All Your Needs

"We have twenty-seven cents and all the promises of God."
~Hudson Taylor, missionary to China, in a letter to a friend
regarding his prayer for more missionaries[1]

Read Philippians 4:14–23.

As Paul closed his letter, he recounted the multiple times the
Philippians showed him generosity. He assured them he was not
asking for more but wanted to remind them that God, who sees
the heart (Heb. 4:12), knew they had willingly sacrificed on his
behalf and would reward them.

A gift given out of love is "a sweet-smelling aroma, an acceptable sacrifice, well pleasing to God." Generosity is encouraged
repeatedly throughout Scripture and is evidence of love. Amy

Carmichael, a missionary to India, wrote: "You can give without loving, but you cannot love without giving."[2] Because God *loved* the world, he *gave* his only Son (John 3:16). Generosity comes from the heart of God.

Generosity sometimes looks one-sided, but Proverbs 11:24–25 says:

> Give freely and become more wealthy;
> be stingy and lose everything.
> The generous will prosper;
> those who refresh others will themselves be refreshed.

These verses are truisms — they are generally true most of the time. Being generous does not guarantee that you will become wealthy, but God rewards Christian generosity in this life and in eternity. The Philippians chose to store their treasure in heaven (Matt. 6:20) through their generosity, instead of hoarding their money and disregarding the needs of others.

The Philippians had physical needs, so Paul reminded them that God would supply them. One of God's names is *Jehovah-Jireh*, which means "the LORD will provide" (Gen. 2:11–14). Paul's confidence in God's provision rested in God's nature. He gives out of His riches in glory, which are limitless. He owns cattle on a thousand hills (Ps. 50:10), and the whole world belongs to him. He put a coin in a fish's mouth (Matt. 17:24–27) and allowed the oil to flow for a poor widow and her sons (2 Kings 4:1–7). God feeds the sparrows and dresses the lilies of the field (Matt. 6:25–34). And he cares much more for his children!

DEAR MISSIONARY, you are probably constantly being asked to give of yourself spiritually through counsel, advice, and prayer or financially to those around you. The demands on your time, attention, and finances never stop, and it may feel like you are always on the giving end. Don't allow bitterness to take root in your heart. God sees how you are being poured out for others (Phil. 2:17) and will reward you. You cannot out-give God—those who refresh others will be refreshed. God will not let your cup run dry.

God knows what you need and promises to supply it. Can you hold onto this truth when your monthly financial support drops or your funding sources dry up? Can you trust him when he seems to ignore what *you think* you need most?

God knows what we need most. Sometimes, we need to learn patience or, like Paul, to be content. If you are experiencing a lack in your life, perhaps God is calling you to trust him as you wait on him.

Your modeling of contentment, wholehearted trust, and dependence on the Lord may be what God uses to draw others closer to him, or God's miraculous provision in your situation may turn someone's heart from doubt to belief.

God will either supply you the strength through Christ Jesus to be content, or he will supply your needs. Let him fill your needs in his way and his timing. He *will* do it. Through it all, whether in lack or abundance, rejoice and declare with Paul that God, our Father, deserves glory forever and ever.

Amen!

DEEP DIVE:

1) Read Proverbs 19:17 and Matthew 25:31–40. How do these Scriptures teach you to view your giving?

_____

_____

_____

_____

2) What does 2 Corinthians 9:6–15 teach about giving? What is the outcome of generosity in these verses?

_____

_____

_____

_____

3) Revisit the story of Elijah when he was on the run from King Ahab and Queen Jezebel in 1 Kings 17:1–16. List all the ways God provided for him. What does this demonstrate about God?

_____

_____

_____

_____

Day 30: Your Job Description

"Those who teach by their doctrine must teach by their life, else
they pull down with one hand what they build up with the
other."
~Matthew Henry[1]

Read Philippians 3:17 and 4:9.

"Brothers, join in imitating me, and keep your eyes
on those who walk according to the example you
have in us" (Phil. 3:17).

"What you have learned and received and heard and
seen in me—practice these things, and the God of
peace will be with you" (Phil. 4:9).

DEAR MISSIONARY, this is your job description. Wherever God has placed you and in whatever capacity he uses you, you must remember that you are being watched. Your behavior will speak louder than your words. If you are not living what you preach, you will hinder the gospel instead of promoting it.

Charles Spurgeon said:

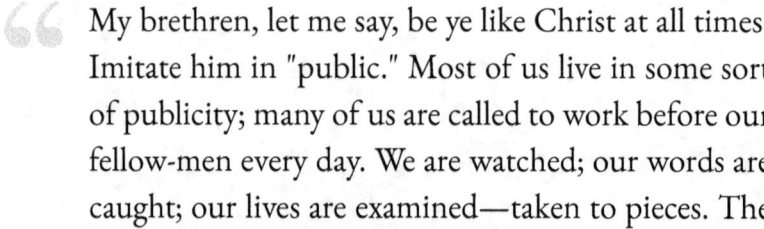

> My brethren, let me say, be ye like Christ at all times. Imitate him in "public." Most of us live in some sort of publicity; many of us are called to work before our fellow-men every day. We are watched; our words are caught; our lives are examined—taken to pieces. The eagle-eyed, argus-eyed world observes everything we do, and sharp critics are upon us. Let us live the life of Christ in public.[2]

Some aspects of theology may be beyond a person's understanding, but everyone recognizes bad behavior, abusive words, and an impure lifestyle. We need to show people what Christianity looks like. Do not underestimate the power of a life lived by the Spirit. I will leave you with one true story from a refugee camp in Uganda.

A team of Americans lived among the Sudanese refugees, hoping to reach them with the gospel. Though they tried, making a connection with the Sudanese people was challenging. One day, a sudden rain pour caught the team's laundry outside, drying on the clothesline. One of the young men ran out and began collecting the clothes to save them from the rain while the dumbfounded Sudanese watched. Men do not do any kind of "housework" in Sudanese culture.

Later, a Muslim Sudanese woman who had observed the young man's behavior approached one of the American women to share her thoughts on what she had witnessed. "I can tell that your men really love you and love this God you have been telling us about because they take the laundry down for you when you are out and it rains."[3]

This simple act helped open an opportunity to explain that Christians love and serve each other the way Christ loved and served us.

The team's ability to minister among the refugees changed that day because a young man lived out his faith in service to his teammates. A godly life is a powerful form of preaching.

Dear missionary, can you, in good conscience, say, "Do as I do"?

You may recognize you have a long way to go before you are comfortable setting yourself forth as an example, but remember that "he who began a good work in you will be faithful to complete it" (Phil. 1:6).

"Let your conduct be worthy of the gospel of Christ" (Phil. 1:27). Then you will shine like a city on a hill (Matt. 5:14) and make the most of every opportunity (Col. 4:5).

When you fail, keep "pressing on toward the goal" and make knowing Christ your greatest passion. If you value Christ above everything else and seek to love the Lord with all your heart, soul, mind, and strength (Mark 12:30), you will live a life worth emulating.

"Now may the Lord of peace himself give you peace at all times in every way. The Lord be with you all" (2 Thess. 3:16).

DEEP DIVE:

1) Read 1 Timothy 4:12. What was Timothy told to do?

_____

_____

_____

_____

2) Read 1 Thessalonians 1:2–10. Who did the Thessalonians imitate? As they lived godly lives, who did they become examples for?

_____

_____

_____

_____

3) Discipleship is essential. All of us need to have a mentor and people we are mentoring. Can you identify, by name, the people who fill these roles in your life? Write them below. If you cannot, *get busy* finding someone who can pour into you and others you can pour into.

_____

_____

_____

_____

Want More?

SAUL THE ZEALOT, PAUL THE MISSIONARY

Want to learn more about the Apostle Paul and the incredible life and ministry he had?

Head over to my website, **janayabale.com** and click on the tab labeled "Freebies" to grab your free copy of my Bible study, *Saul the Zealot, Paul the Missionary*.

It covers Paul's background, conversion to Christianity, calling to the ministry, and first, second, and third missionary journeys.

Great for solo study or for a Bible study group, after completing *Saul the Zealot, Paul the Missionary*, you will never look at Paul the same way again.

THE GREAT COMMISSION QUIZ

How well do you know the great commission? Test your knowledge with a free quiz. You can access the quiz from my website by clicking on the tab that says "Great Commission Quiz."

LEAVE A REVIEW

If this book blessed and encouraged you, would you consider leaving a written review on the platform where you purchased it?

Reviews help others discover the book and be willing to give it a chance.

I appreciate it so much!

Resources

The following are some online Bible study resources. Some of these websites have corresponding phone or tablet applications.

BIBLE TRANSLATIONS IN THOUSANDS OF LANGUAGES

These are both excellent resources for missionaries as they have Bible translations for thousands of languages. Some also include audio recordings of the Scriptures.

Faith Comes by Hearing
    faithcomesbyhearing.com (read/listen online)
    Bible.is (app)

YouVersion
Youversion.com (information regarding the app)
Bible.com (for online use)

RESEARCH TOOLS, LEXICONS, AND COMMENTARIES

Blue Letter Bible
blueletterbible.org (web and app)

Bible Gateway
biblegateway.com (web and app)

Bible Study Tools
biblestudytools.com (web use only)

BIBLE SOFTWARE (REQUIRE PURCHASE)

Logos
logos.com (online and app)

Accordance Bible Software
accordancebible.com (online and app)

Disclaimer: I have not personally used all of the resources these websites/apps offer. Some include commentaries, sermon notes, articles, and other curricula that I have not researched. The views expressed therein are theirs, not mine. Use discernment.

About the Author

Janay Abale is an author, speaker, Bible teacher, and pastor's wife. She lives in rural Uganda, where she has been a missionary for over ten years. She often has to stop homeschooling her four children to chase the monkeys and baboons out of her backyard.

Janay Abale holding a monkey

Janay never goes anywhere without a book. She adds things

she has already finished to her "to-do" list just to get the satisfaction of crossing them off. She enjoys the three C's: coffee, cheese, and chocolate (when she can get them). She enjoys ministry to women, teen girls, and children and leads the women's ministry at her church.

You can join her newsletter at janayabale.com.

Acknowledgments

All glory, honor, praise, and thanks must first go to Jesus Christ, my Savior, without whom the world and my life would be meaningless. You redeemed my soul and gave me a purpose worth living for. Truly, my boundary lines have fallen in pleasant places and my heart rejoices that you have made known to me the paths of life (Ps. 16).

Thank you to my parents, who didn't choose to be missionary parents but have risen to the occasion in myriad ways. I couldn't be *here* if you weren't *there*. You raised me to know Jesus and gave me the greatest gift possible through our family heritage of faith.

Thank you to my King Bosco, a genuine diamond in the rough, a man among men, and the cream of the crop. I'm better in every way because of you. Your support and influence have been invaluable. Thank you for letting me invest my time and our finances in making this book a reality.

Thank you to my dear children, Jazzlyn, Jade, Josiah, and

Jubilee, for being patient when Mommy spent too much time on the computer. You are the four loves of my heart.

Thank you, beta readers, for wading through the unpolished edition of this book and giving invaluable feedback that made it so much better:

- Amanda Kirbara
- Kevin and Angela Blank
- Heidi Bukeera
- Anne Brit Sukka Tiriwa
- Heather Dingess
- Rachael Henderson
- Tim Ownby
- Medeline Onzima

Thank you to everyone who has supported me and my family and our missionary work financially and through prayer. Your partnership has kept us on the field and encouraged us tremendously.

Editing: Teresa Crumpton of authorspark.org

Book cover design: 100 Covers. 100covers.com

Notes

BACKGROUND FOR THE BOOK OF PHILIPPIANS

1. D.A. Carson and Douglas J. Moo, *Introducing the New Testament*, ed. Andrew David Naselli (Grand Rapids: Zondervan, 2010), 108.

DAY 1: PLANTING THE PHILIPPIAN CHURCH

1. *The Westminster Collection of Christian Quotations* (United States: Westminster John Knox Press, 2001), 120.

DAY 2: JOYFUL SURRENDER

1. Jim Elliot, *The Journals of Jim Elliot* (Grand Rapids: Revell, 2002), 173-174.

DAY 4: THE PROMISE OF COMPLETION

1. Amy Carmichael, *If: What Do I Know of Calvary Love?* (United States: Christian Literature Crusade), 1938.

DAY 5: A PRAYER FOR GROWTH

1. "Though references to this quote are ubiquitous and always attributed to Zwemer, no original source document could be found." Daniel Akin et al., *40 Questions about the Great Commission* (Grand Rapids, Kregel, 2020), 295.

DAY 6: GOD'S PURPOSES ARE NEVER THWARTED

1. Quoted in Billy Graham, *Unto the Hills: A Daily Devotional* (Nashville: Thomas Nelson, 2010), 17.

DAY 7: RIVALRY ON THE MISSION FIELD

1. Courtney Anderson, *To the Golden Shore: The Life of Adoniram Judson* (Grand Rapids: Zondervan, 1972), 334.

DAY 8: ATTITUDE OF TRIUMPH

1. Timothy Keller, *Prayer: Experiencing Awe and Intimacy with God.* (United States: Penguin Publishing Group, 2016), 18.

DAY 9: CITIZEN OF HEAVEN

1. *The Westminster Collection of Christian Quotations.* (United States: Westminster John Knox Press, 2001), 165.

DAY 10: STAND FIRM WITHOUT FEAR

1. Brother Yun, et al., *Back to Jerusalem: Three Chinese House Church Leaders Share Their Vision to Complete the Great Commission* (United Kingdom: Intervarsity Press, 2012), 58.
2. Dwight L. Moody, *The New Sermons of Dwight Lyman Moody* (New York: Goodspeed, 1880), 342.

DAY 11: THE GIFT OF SUFFERING

1. *Perspectives on the World Christian Movement (4th Edition): A Reader.* (N.p.: William Carey Publishing, 2009).
2. Walvoord, John F., and Roy B. Zuck, Dallas Theological Seminary. *The Bible Knowledge Commentary: An Exposition of the Scriptures.* Wheaton, IL: Victor Books, 1985.

DAY 12: MIND OF CHRIST

1. George MacDonald, *Unspoken Sermons* (London: Longmans, Green, and Co., 1907), 135.

DAY 13: EVERY KNEE WILL BOW

1. John Piper, *Let the Nations Be Glad! The Supremacy of God in Missions* (United States: Baker Publishing Group), 2010
2. Dag Heward-Mills, *Fundamentals of Evangelism* (N.p.: Parchment House, 2016), 128.
3. Russell T. Hitt, *Jungle Pilot: The Life and Witness of Nate Saint* (Grand Rapids: Discovery House, 1959), 158.

DAY 14: HIS WILL

1. Regina D. Sullivan, *Lottie Moon*, (Baton Rouge, LA: LSU Press, 2011), 150-154.
2. A.W. Tozer, "Four Ways to Find God's Will," *HIS Magazine*, May 1969, 9.
3. *The Complete Works of C. H. Spurgeon*, Volume 32: Sermons 1877-1937. (N.p.: Delmarva Publications, Inc., 2015).

DAY 15: SHINE

1. Billy Graham, *Wisdom for Each Day* (Nashville: Thomas Nelson, 2008), 168.
2. Matthew Henry, *Matthew Henry's Commentary on the Whole Bible: Complete and Unabridged in One Volume.* (Peabody: Hendrickson, 1994).

DAY 16: POURED OUT

1. Oswald Chambers, *My Utmost For His Highest* (Grand Rapids: Discovery House Publishers, 1992), Feb. 2.

DAY 17: FAITHFUL, FOCUSED, AND WILLING

1. Russell R. Cook, *Daily Devotions for Deacons: 260 Instructional and Inspirational Devotions* (United Kingdom: WestBow Press, 2015).

DAY 18: VARIETY FOR GOD'S GLORY

1. Timothy Keller, *Shaped by the Gospel: Doing Balanced, Gospel-Centered Ministry in Your City* (United States: Zondervan, 2016), 18.

DAY 19: PUT NO CONFIDENCE IN THE FLESH

1. Charles Haddon Spurgeon, *Devotional Classics of C. H. Spurgeon* (United States: Sovereign Grace Publishers, Incorporated), 2000.

DAY 20: TO KNOW CHRIST

1. Watchman Nee, *In His Own Words* (N.p.: Raymond Wells, 2021).
2. Quoted in Daniel Akin et al., *40 Questions about the Great Commission* (Grand Rapids, Kregel, 2020), 295.
3. William MacDonald, *Believer's Bible Commentary* (United States: Thomas Nelson, 2008).

DAY 21: PRESS ON

1. A. W. Tozer, *The Pursuit of God* (N.p.: Gideon House Books, 2017).
2. Eugene Peterson, *A Long Obedience in the Same Direction: Discipleship in an Instant Society* (Downers Grove, IL: InterVarsity Press, 2019).

DAY 22: DON'T LOSE GROUND

1. I.D.E. Thomas, *A Puritan Golden Treasury* (Carlisle, PA: Banner of Truth, 2000), 191.

DAY 23: ENEMIES OF CHRIST

1. Oswald Chambers, *Biblical Ethics—The Moral Foundation of Life: The Philosophy of Sin—Ethical Principles of the Christian Life* (United Kingdom: Discovery House Publishers, 1998).
2. Robert L. Thomas, *New American Standard Hebrew-Aramaic and Greek Dictionaries:Updated Edition.* (Anaheim: Foundation Publications, Inc.), 1998.
3. William MacDonald, *Believer's Bible Commentary: Old and New Testaments.* (Nashville: Thomas Nelson, 1995).

DAY 24: AGREE WITH EACH OTHER IN THE LORD

1. The Complete Works of C. H. Spurgeon, Volume 11: Sermons 607 to 667. N.p.: Delmarva Publications, Inc., (n.d.).
2. This term can also be translated as a proper name. Though this man is not named, some believe it refers to Epaphroditus.
3. F. F. Bruce, *New International Bible Commentary*. (Grand Rapids, MI: Zondervan Publishing House, 1979).

DAY 25: REJOICE

1. Billy Graham, "Peace with God: The Secret of Happiness" (United States: Thomas Nelson, 2011).
2. A.B. Simpson, *Days of Heaven Upon Earth* (Nyack, NY: Christian Alliance Publishing Company, 1897), 104.

DAY 26: THE PATH TO PEACE

1. Amy Carmichael, *Candles in the Dark: Letters of Amy Carmichael* (Fort Washington, PA: Christian Literature Crusade, 1982), 53.
2. "Charles H. Spurgeon Quotes," Quote Fancy, Accessed September 23, 2023, https://quotefancy.com/charles-h-spurgeon-quotes.

DAY 27: THINK

1. *The Westminster Collection of Christian Quotations* (United States: Westminster John Knox Press, 2001), 315.

DAY 28: CONTENTMENT

1. Elisabeth Elliot, *Keep A Quiet Heart*, (Ann Arbor, MI: Servant Publications, 1995), 21.

DAY 29: HE WILL SUPPLY ALL YOUR NEEDS

1. "J. Hudson Taylor: God's Mighty Man of Prayer," Wholesome Words,

Accessed September 22, 2023, https://www.wholesomewords.org/missions/biotaylor3.html.

2. *The Westminster Collection of Christian Quotations* (United States: Westminster John Knox Press, 2001), 122.

DAY 30: YOUR JOB DESCRIPTION

1. Matthew Henry, *Matthew Henry's Commentary on the Whole Bible: Complete and Unabridged in One Volume* (Peabody: Hendrickson Publishers, 1994).

2. "Christ's People—Imitators of Him," The Spurgeon Center, Accessed October 9, 2023, https://www.spurgeon.org/resource-library/sermons/christs-people-imitators-of-him.

3. This story was narrated to me by Rob and Heidi Douglass.

www.ingramcontent.com/pod-product-compliance
Lightning Source LLC
Chambersburg PA
CBHW071257130626
46556CB00003B/1351